A FORGE OF
FREEDOM BOOK

The Thirteen Colonies
~1763~

MILES
0   50   100   200

N
W   E
S

Ticonderoga

N.H.

Portsmouth
Boston
Plymouth

NEW YORK

Albany

MASS.

Hartford
CONN.
New Haven

R.I.
Newport
Providence

N.Y.

PENNSYLVANIA

N.J.

New York City

Trenton
Philadelphia   Burlington
Wilmington

Baltimore
Annapolis

DEL.
MD.
MD.

VIRGINIA

Richmond
Williamsburg
Jamestown

ATLANTIC OCEAN

NORTH CAROLINA

Charlotte   New Bern

SOUTH CAROLINA

Wilmington

Charleston

GEORGIA

Savannah

RIKI

The New York Colony

by

Thelma Nurenberg

CROWELL-COLLIER PRESS
Collier-Macmillan Limited, London

To Carla and John

Library of Congress Catalog Card Number: 77–77966

The Macmillan Company
Collier-Macmillan Canada Ltd., Toronto, Ontario
Printed in the United States of America

FIRST PRINTING

PICTURE CREDITS
Brown Brothers, 33, 34–35, 67, 111, Culver Pictures, Inc.,
20–21, 36, 53, 62, 64, 97, 104; Historical Pictures Service—Chicago,
6, 7, 8, 10–11, 14, 16, 23, 28, 30, 31, 38, 42, 46–47, 49, 50, 55, 60,
70, 73, 74, 81, 84, 86, 94, 95, 106–107, 114, 120.

Contents

The
New York
Colony

Chapter 1:

The First Settlers

The ancestors of the American Indians left Asia some twenty thousand years ago at about the time the Ice Age ended. They crossed the Bering Strait, which was then dry land, to Alaska. In the course of time, freezing weather, scarcity of food, and long months without sunlight drove them south and then east across the Rocky Mountains and along the plains. Some settled there. Others wandered on.

About six thousand years ago the first groups reached the region later known as New York. They found a land of forests, vast lakes, long, winding rivers, hills, and tree-studded mountains. Fish were plentiful in the streams and lakes, and there were wild ducks in the marshes, grouse and turkey in the thick brush. The forests abounded with deer, elk, and bear and with smaller animals, such as beaver, muskrat, woodchuck, raccoon, and squirrel.

The Indians settled there, choosing land along the banks of lakes and rivers. They built houses of saplings that they drove into the ground, bending the tops over into an arch, covering roof and frame with sheets of bark and mats of rushes. Holes were left in the roof to let out smoke from the cooking. Smaller houses, in which individual families lived, were built around a "longhouse," which was one hundred feet in length and housed several families, each with separate cooking fires and dishes. Other longhouses were used for ceremonial purposes and for tribal conferences.

By this time the Indians had developed a civilization, a religion, and a tribal government.

The women worked the soil and vegetables grew in abundance because the soil, fed by the many streams, was rich. They tended the young plants with hoes made from the shoulder bone of wolf or deer and twined the bean vine around the corn stalk. They also raised pumpkins and squash between the rows of corn.

The forest furnished the tribes not only with game, but also wood for canoes, dishes, barrels, and fuel. The skins of animals were tanned and made into clothing and shoes. They made tools out of stone, wood, and animal bones, and they used flint to make spears and arrowheads.

Although each village grew or made nearly everything that was needed, they traded with other tribes for what they lacked. This was done on a barter basis, or by an exchange of furs, flint, foodstuffs, and wampum. The latter was made by the Long Island Indians from pearly clam shells that were skilfully clipped, rubbed smooth, and woven into belts. Wampum was used as money or ornaments.

Every ten years or so a tribe moved because the soil had lost its richness and game as well as fish had been used up. They traveled on lakes or rivers, which were their water highways, to the north, the south, and the west. The Iroquois and the Algonquins settled on or near what is now Manhattan.

Women had an important role in Indian life. They controlled the lands of their sizable family. The oldest woman was considered the mother of the entire family, which consisted of grandparents, uncles, aunts, fathers, mothers, and of course, the children. The women chose the chiefs who handled the daily affairs, while the braves chose their own war chiefs.

Each tribe had its own governing council. Laws such as ours did not exist for them; they had customs that they followed, and those who broke them were punished. Crime was rare among the Indians. If a man stole anything, he had to give his own property to the man from whom he had stolen. If there was a murder, the family of the victim could demand the life of the murderer.

The Indians believed that people, animals, birds, plants, trees, and objects had a spirit. They worshiped the Great Spirit in heaven, and prayed to keep the Evil Spirit from sending a drought or a flood that would destroy their crops. They also prayed to the Great Spirit not to aid their enemies.

Events such as a hunt were celebrated by the ceremonial dances. As they danced they chanted, calling on the spirits of animals to give them food so that their people would not starve; they did not kill for sport, but only for their needs.

The Indians were artistic; their clothing and footwear were beaded and ornamented, their eating earthenware beautifully designed. They were intelligent and ahead of the Europeans in the knowledge of preserving food by salting fish and meat. They were inventive in the way they shaped tools and weapons out of stone, flint, bone, and wood.

They had a rich folklore and loved to listen to the old

men of the tribe tell stories about how the world began, of the stars, the sun (their great elder brother), animals, mountains, their war heroes, and the struggles of Hiawatha.

Why has the chipmunk stripes down his back? Listen as the old Seneca chief tells it:

> A hungry bear could find nothing to eat. One day he caught a chipmunk. He was about to eat it when the chipmunk begged for a chance to dance once more and sing his death chant. The bear set him down but watched very closely. The chipmunk sang about his wish to escape, and danced back and forth over the leaves. He found what he was looking for, a soft spot that meant there was a hole under the leaves. He darted into it. But the bear struck him with his paw and tore the skin right down the back of the chipmunk.
>
> He escaped, but the chipmunk had stripes down his back ever after.

Although group of the Algonquin tribes lived peacefully among themselves, they fought other tribes for one reason or another. But all the tribes suffered alike when the powerful Iroquoian tribes from north of the Great Lakes (Canada) attacked, destroying villages, killing men, women, and children.

At that time (about 1570) there lived among the Onondagas a man whom all the Indians trusted and to whom they went for advice. His name was Hiawatha, which means "a very wise man," the legendary hero of Henry W. Longfellow's poem.

Hiawatha advised the Indians to call the tribes together. He told them that their only safety was in uniting into one band of brothers. The five tribes should have "one voice, one fire, one pipe, and one war club." He told them that if the five tribes ceased fighting each other, the Great Spirit would make them happy and prosperous.

The five Iroquois tribes of what is now central and western New York formed a confederation with one set of rules that governed all: "The object of these laws is to establish peace between the numerous nations of Indians, hostility will be done away with, for the preservation and protection of life, property, and liberty. . . . and when the Five Nation Confederation chiefs assemble to hold a council . . . they will offer thanks to the Great Spirit that dwells in heaven above, the source and ruler of our lives, and it is him that sends daily blessings upon us, our daily wants, and daily health, and they will then declare the council open for the transaction of business, and give decisions of all that is done in the council." The council was empowered to declare war and to send and receive ambassadors. (Later you will see how the French and English courted these Indian chiefs as allies in their wars in America.)

The Indians led a simple, natural existence, varied by the excitements of the hunt and the occasional tribal conflicts, until the morning they woke and saw the strange ships in the harbor. It changed their fate forever.

The Indians Meet the White Men

For more than a hundred years the Europeans had been trying to find a shorter route to India and China to obtain their rare gems, ivories, silks, velvets, and spices. In 1497 Henry VII of England gave John Cabot permission to sail to the west in search of new lands and a new route to the Orient. He came to a land twenty-one hundred miles from England and sailed along the coast for about nine hundred miles. This voyage gave the English their claim to the land from Labrador to Florida.

Italian-born Amerigo Vespucci sailed from Portugal and reached American shores on August 7 (or 17), 1501; the continent received its name from him. Verrazano made the

An Indian Village on Manhattan Island in the early seventeenth century

same discovery in 1524, as did a Negro explorer from Portugal, Estavan Gomez. He had been Magellan's chief pilot. In 1525 Charles of Spain sent him to explore the eastern shores of America. He reached the site of New York on January 17, 1526. He was the first European who bore evidence of having sailed to the shores of Maine, and his chart of the voyage is considered the most valuable yet drawn. There is a draft of it in the British Museum.

None of these explorers stepped onto the land of the great continent that they kept skirting, but Henry Hudson did. In 1609 the Dutch East India Company sent out this Englishman to discover a shorter passageway to the Orient. He left Holland and sailed north and into the icy Arctic Ocean. He turned back. He saw a river that stretched far inland of the great land mass of the American coast and thought it a waterway that cut through to the Pacific Ocean. On September 13, 1609, Hudson sailed the *Half-Moon* into the waters of what is now New York harbor. He ordered his men to lower a small boat and sent them ashore to investigate.

From the shore came two canoes filled with Indians dressed in furs and feathers. They were eager to know who these strangers were and what they wanted. One of the Indians raised his bow and arrow and an English sailor named John Coleman fell. The crew on the ship did not fire back as it had begun to rain and the Indians retreated.

The next morning Hudson sailed the *Half-Moon* into the upper bay into which Manhattan Island juts out. Canoes filled with Indians rowed out and they were friendly. The white men traded axes, knives, mirrors, and red cloth for beaver and other furs. The Indians and the white men were pleased with their bartering.

Friendly Indians paddled out to meet the Half-Moon

The *Half-Moon* traveled farther up the river (now the Hudson) and then, on October 4, set sail for Holland. The next year other ships came from the Dutch East India Company and traded with the Indians. Furs, which were in great demand in Europe, were exchanged for beads, blankets, kettles, knives, and tools.

Then, in about 1614, the Dutch came again and built a few huts on the tip of the island to be used as a trading post. Farther along the river they put up a log fort and called it Fort Orange (Albany) and traded with the Indians. They named the land along the river New Netherland.

One of the Dutch ships, the *Tiger,* caught fire near Manhattan Island and burned. The sailors swam to shore, and befriended by the Indians who taught them to hunt, they lived safely through the winter. In the spring the sailors built another boat, the *Restless*. It was too small to cross the ocean, and so the captain, Adrian Block, explored

In 1614 the Dutch built a few huts on the tip of Manhattan Island to be used as a trading post

the waterways that surrounded the island. Presently another ship came from Holland, and after the trading, set sail for home, taking the sailors with them.

In 1624 a larger ship arrived with thirty families who had come to stay. They had been sent by the newly formed Dutch West India Company under a charter granted by the Dutch government that gave the Company the right to control all the trade by the Dutchmen along the eastern coasts of North America and South America and the western coast of Africa.

Not all these first colonists were Dutch. Some were Walloons, French-speaking Protestants who had fled to Holland to escape religious persecution, just as the Pilgrims had fled England for the same reason and settled in Holland. A few families were left on Manhattan, and then the boat sailed off to Fort Orange, where the rest of the passengers settled.

In Manhattan the Indians helped the newcomers build log huts inside the walls of the fort, taught them to hunt, and when the food gave out, provided them with corn and beans. Without this help the colonists could not have survived that first winter in the wilderness of the New World.

The next year four more ships arrived, the *Cow,* the *Horse,* the *Pig,* and the *Sheep,* carrying these animals and more settlers. The Indians looked on excitedly as the animals were unloaded, for, other than dogs, they had never seen such animals before.

Peter Minuit, the First Governor, Arrives

The Dutch West India Company sent Peter Minuit to be the director of the colony. He reached Manhattan on May 4, 1626. Judging by his record, he was a good and able man who believed in fair and honest dealing with the Indians as well as with the colonists. He summoned the leading Indian chiefs to a conference and told them he wanted to barter for their island. He offered goods valued at about sixty guilders ($24), which consisted of beads, knives, and farming tools. The Indians accepted, and the island became Dutch property. It was called New Amsterdam. In a report to the Dutch West India Company, the island was described as a "narrow, rocky point of land, purling brooks and broken by ocean inlets; a chain of low hills in the background covered with forests of hickory and chestnut; valleys sheltering maize fields and wigwams; wide marshes beyond which roamed wolves and panthers."

The Indians accepted Peter Minuit's barter offer, and Manhattan Island became Dutch property

Governing the colony was an advisory council of five members who were appointed in Amsterdam, where its laws were made. But the governor and the council could make local laws, which the Company had to approve.

By 1626 the colony consisted of about thirty small huts with thatched roofs. They were clustered inside or close to the fort, near what is now Albany, which was being rebuilt by African slaves brought in by the Company. At this time there were about two hundred Dutch, Walloon, and English settlers. They were provided with as much land as they could farm and were exempt from taxation for ten years. Besides tending their animals, they raised

flax, rye and wheat, corn and vegetables. They also raised tobacco, which the Indians had taught them to plant and cure. They were forbidden to do any manufacturing, nor could they have a permanent title to the land they lived on and worked.

They could trade with other colonies but were not allowed to sell the cloth the women wove except to the Company.

In Fort Orange relations with the Indians were not as good as in Manhattan. Unwisely, the commander involved himself in a war between the Mohicans and Mohawks in which he and three of his men were killed. Governor Minuit hastened to the fort and succeeded in making peace between the colonists and the Indians.

Governor Minuit saw the need to establish friendly relations with the New England colonies and on March 9, 1627, he sent a courier to Governor William Bradford of Plymouth, in which he proposed an exchange of "serviceable Dutch commodities for beaver and other skins or merchandise in which the Plymouth settlers might be disposed to traffic."

Bradford, in his reply, expressed friendship for the people of New Amsterdam, but he hinted that the Dutch were trespassers. (The English did not like having a Dutch colony between Plymouth and Jamestown.)

Not one to be put off by this hint of trespassing, Governor Minuit sent another courier with gifts of cheeses and sugar and a letter proving the rights of the Dutch to their territory. He expressed his wish for friendship and goodwill. Governor Bradford's reply was friendlier, and he requested an ambassador be sent to Plymouth for an adjustment of their boundary lines. There were disputes with other colonies over boundaries, but the settlers continued to trade with each other.

More people came. They were Germans, French, English,

and Scots. Few Dutch people left their homeland at that time. Holland was then the most prosperous country in Europe, and the Dutch enjoyed religious and political liberties that were denied elsewhere.

To induce the Dutch to settle in New Amsterdam, the Company offered vast tracts of land to any member of the Company who, at his own expense and within four years, would found a colony of fifty adults. The founder was given the title of patroon, which means patron or protector. He had to buy the land from the Indians and was free to trade in everything except furs.

The patroon had the rights of a feudal lord. The settlers were bound to his service for a certain period. The patroon paid for preparing the land, building houses and barns, and received a fixed rental in stock or produce. The farmers were protected from the Indians by the patroon, who provided for the support of a minister and a schoolmaster.

The settlement on Manhattan Island grew and prospered. At first church services had been held in the mill loft, but it was soon too small for the settlers. In 1633 the first church was built with Company funds. It was a plain wooden building that served as a schoolhouse as well. The first schoolmaster, Adam Roelantsen, had to take in washing to help support himself. According to old court records, in 1638 he sued a colonist named Gillies for nonpayment of fees due him for the washing of his linen.

Soon houses of brick were built, with steep gables, surrounded by gardens and vegetable patches. Orchards were planted with a variety of fruit trees.

Indians roamed the little town and mingled freely with the settlers. The Dutch women thought the Indian women dirty because they smelled of the bear grease they rubbed on their faces to keep off the flies and mosquitoes. The Indian women could not understand why the Dutch were so fussy about scrubbing floors daily and washing clothes

The settlement on Manhattan Island grew and prospered

frequently. They were very impressed with the blue and white tiled stoves decorated with pictures of windmills and flowers; the chairs and the tables; the handsome carved wooden boxes that held linens and dresses; the safes that held salted meat. Their own, smoked, hung in dry strips inside the roof of their wigwams.

The Indian women marveled at all this, but it was they who taught the white women how to shell the corn, dry it, and pound it into meal for winter use.

Of course they were fascinated by the silk stuff some of the Dutch had, but they did wonder why these women labored so hard at carding and spinning thread that they then wove into cloth when skins were had so easily and their own tanned deerskin dresses were so soft and ornamented.

Nor could they understand why the insides of the houses were so sparkling clean while the outsides were heaped with rubbish. Cows, sheep, and pigs ran about and were even battering down the wooden walls of the fort!

Although the settlement was growing, the number of farms failed to keep pace with it; it was easier for some settlers to trade than to clear land and farm. Without realizing that they were storing up trouble for the future, they made rum that they sold to the Indians. The chiefs begged the white chief not to let it be sold as the Indians were not used to strong drink—it made them act wildly. Then, too, the traders exchanged muskets and powder for furs. The governor forbade this, but it went on. Furs had become the gold of the New World.

Proof of the extent of this fur trade can be seen in a letter in the Royal Archives at the Hague. It is from Peter Jans Schaghen, Deputy in the States General of Holland, to the officials of the Dutch West India Company. It was written in 1626, and it reads:

High Mighty Sirs:
Here arrived the Ship "The Arms of Amsterdam" which sailed from New Netherland out of the Mauritius (Hudson) River on September 23. They report that our people there are of good courage and live peaceably. They have bought the island Manhattan from the wild men for the value of sixty guilders. It is eleven thousand morgens in extent. They sowed all their grain in the middle of May, and harvested it in the middle of August. They send thence samples of summer grain such as wheat, rye, barley, oats, buckwheat, canary seed, beans and flax.

The cargo of the aforesaid ship is:
7,246 beaver skins
178 1/2 otter skins
675 otter skins
48 mink skins
36 wild cat skins
33 mink skins
34 rat skins

The colonists sometimes traded rum to the Indians in exchange for furs

many logs of oak and nut wood (hickory).

Herewith, be ye High Mighty Sirs commended to the Almighty's grace.

In Amsterdam, Nov. 5, 1626.

Your high mighty's obedient,
P. Schaghen

As you can see, the Indians had been very busy in the year 1626 hunting and skinning animals. Fur was in such great demand by Europeans that four wars were later fought between the English and the French to capture this trade as well as the lands of America.

Wouter van Twiller, the second governor of New Netherland, was formerly a clerk in the warehouse of the West India Company. He was said to be "deficient in the knowledge of men, inexperienced, incompetent and irresolute." He was also a heavy drinker. Washington Irving called him "the doubter," while New Amsterdam's minister, Everhardus Bogardus, referred to him as "a child of Satan," against whom he would preach "such a sermon as will make him shake in his shoes."

With nothing to recommend him except his being the nephew of Kiliaen van Rensselaer, the most powerful of the patroons, and because of his former low occupation, the burghers held him in contempt. The best that could be said of him was that he tried to repair the fort which was always on the verge of collapse, erected a guard house and barracks within the fort enclosure, erected a bakery, a brewery, a boat house, several barns, and dug a well. He built himself a grand brick mansion and several wooden houses for his subordinates and acquired vast land holdings. Van Twiller treated the Indians fairly well, but managed to antagonize the settlers and caused such confusion with his mismanagement of public affairs that he was replaced by William Kieft in 1638.

Chapter 2:

Governor William Kieft—
How To Lose Friends and Make Enemies

The third governor of New Netherland, William Kieft, arrived in the spring of 1638. He was described as a "waspish and wiry little governor" and "fussy and fiery." From the beginning he was determined to be the sole ruler. Although the settlers, in theory, had the privilege of deciding how many men were to make up his council, Kieft would permit only one representative. He gave the councilman a single vote while he, "to prevent all danger of a tie," kept two votes for himself. From his first act the settlers knew they were saddled with a tyrant.

Governor Kieft saw trouble everywhere and was not capable enough to deal with it. The fort was crumbling, the guns lay dismounted, the vessels in the harbor were unseaworthy, the windmills did not work, and the farms were without farmers.

The settlers had serious complaints: why should they work hard at clearing the forests and plowing and farming when they were denied title to the land? Selling furs, tobacco, and rum was widely practiced and very profitable, as was the sale of muskets and whiskey to the Indians.

Kieft had placards posted on barns and trees and fences forbidding on penalty of death the sale of muskets or powder to Indians. He put heavy fines on the illegal traffic in furs. He angered the settlers by restricting their personal freedom. No one was permitted to leave the island without a passport. This meant that people could no longer travel freely to other colonies to trade. Curfew was at nine o'clock.

Despite all this, more immigrants came. The Company was now offering more inducements than before—a farmer would be brought free to New Netherland where a farm, house, and barn awaited, with as much land as he could work. Also, he would be provided with horses, cows, pigs, and farming tools. The farmer was to pay $200 per year for six years and could own the farm at the end of that period.

The Company sent over carpenters, smiths, coopers to make barrels and casks, and wainwrights to make or repair wagons. As a result of the new policy, the number of bouweries (farms) on Manhattan increased in 1639 from seven to thirty. New Englanders began to move into the colony on Long Island because of its policy of religious tolerance.

Now New Amsterdam began to grow. St. Nicholas Church was built in 1642, and a stone tavern was erected to house traders and visitors from upper New Netherland, New England, and Virginia. Two roads were laid out, one going north through the center of the island and the other along the water front to the ferry from Manhattan to Long Island. Passengers summoned the ferryman by sounding the horn that hung on a tree at either landing. They paid three

stivers in wampum (about six cents) for the ride across.

Despite Kieft's harsh rule, the people prospered. And then the governor began to make blunders that led to serious trouble.

In order to raise funds for the defense of the colony, he decided to tax the Indians for the upkeep of the forts and the garrisons. The Indians refused to pay; the forts gave them no protection. The chiefs said: "If we ceded to you

*Coopers at work
in New Netherland*

the land you occupy, we will yet remain masters of what we have retained." They insisted that the Dutch still owed them for food provided "during the early years of the settlement."

The tax angered the Indians, but they took no action until the governor's next rash move. He accused the Raritan Indians of some petty thefts on Staten Island, although there was no proof that the thieves belonged to this tribe, and demanded compensation. The soldiers killed several Indians and destroyed their crops. The Indians took revenge. They burned farms on Staten Island and killed four farmers. Kieft offered a reward of ten fathoms of wampum for the head of any Raritan Indian, and this incited the Indians of other tribes against the settlers.

At this time another incident further aroused the Indians. Years before an Indian boy had seen his uncle robbed and murdered by several of Governor Minuit's servants and had vowed vengeance. According to Indian custom, a vow of vengeance must be carried out. When the Indian reached manhood, he killed a settler, Claes Smits.

Kieft demanded that the murderer be surrendered. The chief of the Weekquaesgeeks refused on the ground that the youth had the right to avenge his uncle's murder. Fear of an Indian attack mounted in the colony, and the governor was barely restrained from declaring war.

On August 28, 1641, the first popular assembly met and elected twelve men to work with Kieft for the safety and welfare of the colony. This committee agreed that the murder of Claes Smits must be avenged but "God and the opportunity must first be considered." They advised trading with the Indians until the hunting season arrived, when the enemy "would be scattered and could more easily be beaten." They hoped to delay any action until tempers cooled and fears subsided.

Kieft insisted on action, but the committee refused. Ignoring them, he sent eighty men against the Weekquaesgeeks, "but the guide lost his way and the commander his temper," wrote a chronicler of the times. The party turned back. Alarmed by the threat of attacks, the Indians sued for peace. Kieft insisted that the murderer of Claes Smits be surrendered. A treaty was arranged, but the murderer was not given up. The troubles began anew and spread.

Other peace treaties were signed and broken, more often

by the governor than by the Indians, and this resulted in the worst massacres in the colony.

The Mohawks chose this time to attack the river Indians who went for protection to the Dutch settlements in Pavonia and Corlear's Hook on Manhattan Island. Several hundred of them encamped there. The settlers thought that by sheltering the Indians they would gain their friendship, but Kieft thought otherwise and struck the long delayed blow.

At midnight, February 25, 1643, his soldiers massacred eighty Indian men, women, and children at Pavonia, while at Corlear's Hook forty more were murdered in their sleep. The next morning Kieft welcomed his soldiers, who came bringing the heads of their victims.

Settlers on Long Island attacked the Indians there

News of the two massacres encouraged the settlers on Long Island to attack the Indians there. Now the fire that Kieft had started spread, and warfare raged everywhere.

Fearful that all the settlers and the farms in New Netherland would be wiped out, Kieft again summoned an assembly. Eight men were chosen as councilors, who demanded that efforts be made to pacify the Indians. But the Indians scorned the messengers as "corn thieves" and refused to deal with them.

The farmers whose homes had been burned charged Kieft with responsibility for all the troubles and wanted him sent back to Holland. Kieft shifted the blame on others and this so enraged the people that one of them tried to kill him. The man was shot and his head set upon the gallows. The problems of the settlers were still unsolved.

One morning in the spring of 1643, three delegates from the Indians on Long Island came to Fort Amsterdam with a white flag. Their chief desired the white chief to speak to him at their village on the sea coast.

A planter, De Vries, whose estate on Staten Island had been burned, was considered a friend by the Indians, and one who spoke their language. Together with another settler he went with the Indians to a point near Rockaway, Long Island, where three hundred of the tribe and sixteen chiefs were assembled.

Seating themselves in a circle, the sachems, or chiefs, placed the two white men in the center. Then a chief rose, holding a bundle of small sticks in his hand. He began stating the Indians' grievances, and with each point he made he laid down one stick.

When the Dutch arrived, he said, they had often been without food. The Indians had given them corn and beans. Down went one stick on the ground. They had helped them fish and hunt. Down went another stick. How had the Indians been rewarded? The white men had helped themselves to more and more land, without payment. Another stick. The white men had attacked and killed. One more stick joined the pile, and then still more.

De Vries agreed that all that the chief said was true; the white men had acted unjustly. But now it was necessary to make peace so that all could live and get to their spring planting. He urged the chiefs to come with him to the fort to make peace and receive gifts. Some chiefs objected; they could no longer trust the governor. But the Indian chiefs went. Kieft proved himself cunning and miserly and gave them poor gifts. This angered them.

The troubles continued, and Kieft sent ambassadors to New Haven, Connecticut for assistance. They returned with the message that the English "were not satisfied that the war with the Indians was just."

The entire colony seemed in danger of being destroyed. De Vries, having lost everything, left for Holland. He told Kieft that "the murders in which you have shed so much innocent blood will yet be revenged upon your own head." (Later, Kieft was drowned in a shipwreck while returning to Holland.)

A petition to remove Kieft was sent to the Company. "We have no means of defense against a savage foe, and we have a miserable despot to rule over us." One hundred and thirty soldiers were sent in reply.

Kieft continued to rule. He levied taxes and made laws that the settlers opposed. He even made enemies of his supporters. When the minister preached against him, Kieft avenged himself by ordering the soldiers to beat on drums and fire guns outside the church so that worshipers could not hear the sermon.

The council sent off another letter to the Company describing the desperate situation. They pleaded that either a new governor be sent or that the petitioners be permitted to return to Holland.

The answer came: Kieft was to be recalled and the Indians appeased. The colonists were granted real privileges; the local government was to be vested in a Supreme Council and settlers in towns and villages were to choose deputies to represent them at a semiannual assembly at Manhattan. Manufacturing, which earlier had been forbidden, was allowed and even encouraged. Boundary questions between the Dutch and New Englanders were to be settled. Now fifty-three soldiers were to be maintained at Fort Amsterdam and every settler was commanded to provide himself with a musket.

Kieft was summoned back to Holland to justify himself for the "bloody exploit of February, 1643."

There was great rejoicing over this.

Again Indians appeared at Fort Amsterdam to arrange for a treaty of peace. Kieft wanted to leave one good impression and he not only entered into agreements with the chiefs, but also secured their services as peacemakers with hostile Indians.

Thus, on August 29, 1645, the settlers were summoned by a bell to Fort Amsterdam to hear the articles of the peace treaty: ". . . henceforth no armed Indians were to approach the houses of the colonists and no armed Dutchmen were to visit an Indian village unless with an Indian escort . . ."

The people of the town and the Indians smoked the pipe of peace and pledged eternal friendship. There was peace, and so through diplomacy more was obtained for everyone than Kieft had tried to gain through his wars.

Peter Stuyvesant, the Father with the Big Stick

"He came like a peacock with great state and pomp," wrote a chronicler of his arrival. Salutes from the fort almost exhausted New Amsterdam's supply of powder, while the settlers cheered when the new governor declared: "I shall rule you as a father his children."

This was on May 11, 1647, and it took only a few days for the settlers to realize that he was going to be a very strict father indeed. One month later they were to call him a tyrant.

Washington Irving described him as a "valiant, weather-beaten, mettlesome, obstinate, leathern-sided, lion-hearted old governor."

He was a tough old soldier who had led the Dutch in an attack on the Portuguese island of St. Martin. Wounded in this unsuccessful battle, he lost his right leg and returned to Holland for surgery, after which he wore a leg made of wood bound with silver bands. When he was able to walk again he was appointed governor of New Netherland, where he soon became as famous for his temper as for his wooden leg.

It was an untidy village into which he came, with about seven hundred people living in the one hundred and twenty houses fronted by heaps of refuse, with dirt lanes and tottering fences separating houses that were deep in mud after a rain. Pigs, cows, chickens, and geese roamed every-where and the fort seemed ready to collapse.

Stuyvesant ordered old sheds and fences and ugly pig-pens destroyed. Rubbish had to be carted away and animals as well as poultry were not allowed the run of the town. Seventeen streets were laid out, and some were paved with cobblestones.

Of course the town appearance improved, but tempers did not. The Dutch did not like to be ordered about.

He demanded strict observance of Sunday and forbade liquor to be drawn before and during church services except to travelers. Innkeepers and tapsters were forbidden to keep open after the ringing of the bell at nine every evening and fines were imposed for "drawing a knife or sword rudely or in anger."

He was very strict about proper behavior; when a woman raised her skirts slightly on the muddy road she was brought to court and fined.

As a result of the wars with the Indians, the colony treasury was without funds. Stuyvesant levied taxes on liquor and the export of furs. Two of the Company's ships were ordered to cruise in the West Indies for the purpose of capturing the rich galleons on their way from South America to Spain. The governor was very severe about punishing thieves—the stocks in the fort were rarely empty

The stocks in the fort were rarely empty

—but he did not hesitate to engage in a high form of thievery for the needs of the colony.

Still more money was needed. Stuyvesant told the settlers to choose nine men to help raise taxes. He had no thought of giving them a voice in the government, however, and he rejected their ideas as fast as they were offered. The nine men complained to the Company about the tax on furs they sent to Holland; they were taxed so much that there was little left for their own expenses. Worst of all, they were not allowed a voice in how the money was to be spent or in electing officers to govern them as the people were in Holland.

Word came back that New Amsterdam could choose its own officers, become a city and have a seal. Stuyvesant, however, read the letter his own way—he was the one to choose the officers!

The settlers on Long Island, mainly New Englanders from Connecticut, and those of other settlements met with the leading men of New Amsterdam to draw up a petition for their rights which they would send to Holland. Stuyvesant sent his soldiers to break up the meeting. He forbade anyone to send a petition. "If anyone during my administration shall appeal I will make him a foot shorter and send the pieces to Holland that he may appeal in that way."

The quarrels between the settlers and Stuyvesant went on for about six years. At last Stuyvesant yielded to some of their demands. He decreed that burghers, as well-to-do men were called, could hold office. The five-story inn was turned into a Stadt Huys (City Hall) where the new officers met. When a ruling was made or something was to be announced, a bell was rung and the people gathered to hear the news. Then a notice of it was posted on the wall.

One of the constant dangers that threatened the settlers was fire. The roofs of many houses were thatched and some chimneys were made of logs covered with clay. When

An inn, erected when William Kieft was governor, became the Stadt Huys during Peter Stuyvesant's rule

chimneys became too hot sparks fell on the thatched roof. Stuyvesant ordered that all wooden chimneys be replaced by clay or stone ones and that they be inspected regularly. No haystacks were allowed near a house.

To put the fear of the law into his "children," the governor declared that any man whose house caught fire was careless and must pay a fine!

He ordered one hundred and fifty fire buckets that shoemakers made of leather. Each settler was taxed a beaver skin to pay for them. The leather buckets were placed everywhere and at the cry of "Fire!" the settlers seized them, formed a double line from the nearest well or brook, and the buckets went from hand to hand down the line to the burning house. Back went the empty ones to the well to be filled again.

Stuyvesant dealt justly with the Indians and there was peace, except for a minor incident with a tribe on Staten Island. The governor settled it affably. Quarrels broke out with the New Englanders on Long Island who referred to the Dutch as "their noxious neighbors" and there were boundary disputes with the Connecticut settlers.

To protect the settlers from invasion, Stuyvesant built a high wall across lower Manhattan from east to west. It had two gates through which people came or left and through which the town herdsman drove the cattle to pasture. The gates were closed and locked before nightfall, with a guard before each.

Although the Company favored religious tolerance, Stuyvesant did not. When a group of Jews arrived in 1654, he wrote the Company requesting permission to deport them. The Company refused.

There was only one church in New Amsterdam—the Dutch Reformed. Stuyvesant would not allow any other church to be built. People of other religions could worship freely, but only in their homes! He particularly disliked

A wall was built across lower Manhattan

the Quakers, some of whom he fined, arrested, and deported. He issued a proclamation fining any who gave them hospitality.

Stuyvesant's actions angered the New Englanders of Flushing. They prepared a charter, known as the Flushing Remonstrance, which is the first declaration of religious toleration in America. Stuyvesant was enraged when it was presented to him, and he ordered the messengers arrested.

New Amsterdam was taking on the appearance of a Dutch seaport. Ships anchored in the bay flew the English, Dutch, and French flags. And there were pirate ships, too! Stuyvesant closed an eye to this but the settlers knew, for the sailors were free with their gold pieces and the captains sold oriental shawls, jewels, silks, and other valuables to the merchants.

The town kept growing. Houses began to be built of brick or stone and in 1660 a brickyard was opened. The average value of a two-story dwelling was about $125 and houses rented for about $25 per year. More land was bought from the Indians on Long Island. There were now over one thousand people living in New Amsterdam, and almost as many in all the settlements combined. The city had a mixture of nationalities and eighteen languages were spoken.

Where the world's tallest skyscrapers now stand there was a canal bordered by the houses of the well-to-do. Most were built of brick, two and a half stories high, with steep, sloping, red-tiled roofs.

The *Heere Graft* or principal canal, located just south of where City Hall now stands, was a natural rivulet that had been deepened so that settlers in small boats and Indians in their canoes could ply it. It was spanned by bridges where traders met to barter their wares. In 1676 it was filled in and paved with cobblestones. The jail was inside the fort, and there was almost always someone there

Where New York's skyscrapers now stand there was a canal

in the stocks, being punished because he had been hunting or swearing on Sunday or stealing or being quarrelsome during the week.

School was held in the church. Parents paid the teachers thirty stivers (about sixty cents), or the equivalent in beaver skins, for teaching the younger boys and girls spelling for a quarter term. They paid sixty stivers a quarter for teaching reading, writing, and arithmetic. The poor did not have to pay. The children were taught prayers and psalms and the catechism. Only the boys were taught arithmetic.

The paddle was in frequent use to "put the fear of the Lord" into the children. Each week the children were tested in their catechism and in the sermon the minister had preached.

If school was as tedious as the too-long sermon in an unheated church, there was still plenty of fun to be had. In

A schoolroom in New Amsterdam

winter the children ice-skated on the ponds and slid down
hills on sleds, and in the summer, after the chores, there
was swimming or games to play on the field where the
present City Hall stands.

Despite the many improvements that Old Silver Nails—

one of Stuyvesant's nicknames—made, the people were dissatisfied. They resented Stuyvesant's tyrannical ways. The New Englanders on Long Island were particularly dissatisfied, for they had known home rule in their former colony and wanted it here.

The British Take Over

In September 1664, four British ships anchored at Gravesend Bay. The Dutch were nervous—what did they want? Stuyvesant was at Fort Orange settling some Indian troubles. He hurried back and sent a messenger to Colonel Richard Nicholls, who was in command of the ships, demanding to know why he was in Dutch waters without permission.

The reply enraged the old warrior; he had been ordered to surrender the colony! In Europe the war between the English and the Dutch had already ended—why then this act of war?

Back went the defiant reply: "Never will I surrender!"

The Dutch became concerned when British ships anchored at Gravesend Bay

Nicholls sent another messenger with terms; if the Dutch surrendered they could stay safely and keep their possessions.

Stuyvesant called the town leaders together, but he did not tell the rest of the people the true state of affairs. The leaders realized that the fort was in ruins; there were not enough men and arms to pit against the heavy guns and trained soldiers of the English. As they discussed this, a third British messenger came, with the same terms. Furious, Stuyvesant tore the paper into pieces. The townsfolk must fight!

The presence of four heavily armed ships made the Dutch reluctant to resist. They felt there was no sense in the governor's defiance, no sense in the destruction of the town, nor of people killed.

. A crowd gathered outside the Stadt Huys and demanded to know what terms the British had offered. An official picked up the torn pieces of paper from the floor, put them together, and read aloud the terms that had been offered. The people pleaded for Stuyvesant to yield, but still he refused. His soldiers already saw themselves defeated—and killed. Even the minister said: "It is wrong to shed blood for no purpose!"

Stuyvesant, the old warrior, held out for fighting to the last man and the last bit of powder. Then one of the council handed him a paper. It was from the people massed outside, and it was signed by most of the important burghers; they wanted him to surrender. Among the names was that of his son, Balthazar.

There was no longer any hope. Heartbroken, Stuyvesant said: "I would rather have been carried to my grave." He gave the order to surrender.

The Dutch and the British met at Stuyvesant's farm, The Bouwerie, and discussed terms. Two days later the Dutch

The Dutch and the British met at Stuyvesant's farm to discuss the terms of surrender

soldiers marched out of the fort and their flag came down. The English marched in and raised theirs.

Stuyvesant sailed back to Holland to face charges by the Dutch West India Company for his failure to hold New Netherland. He made a stout defense and blamed the Company for not sending enough soldiers and arms to fight the English.

Then he returned to the town he helped develop and to his beloved Bouwerie, where he died in his eightieth year. His grave is in the grounds of the handsome old church of St. Marks at Second Avenue and Tenth Street, which was the site of the chapel on his country farm.

Chapter 3:

A Charter Is Given and Taken Back

King Charles II of England based his claim to the Dutch colony on the discovery of America in 1497 by John Cabot. It had not been to England's advantage to press that claim earlier. But now it seemed unwise to have the Dutch province separating the New England colonies from the southern ones. Also, Dutch traders made it difficult for England to enforce the Navigation Acts that controlled the trade of her colonies because of all the smuggling that went on between them.

The king gave the colony to his brother James, Duke of York and Albany. New Amsterdam was renamed New York and Fort Orange became Albany. The duke was given power to make the laws, appoint officials, make grants of land, and impose taxes.

Colonel Richard Nicholls became the first royal governor. He was fair in his dealings with the Dutch and the changes he made caused little grumbling. English weights, measures, and money replaced the Dutch, the names of a few streets were changed and the North River became the Hudson River. The Dutch continued to hold important positions in the government.

Oddly enough, it was not the Dutch who troubled the governor but the English on Long Island, as earlier they had troubled Peter Stuyvesant with their demand for religious toleration. They were New Englanders from Connecticut and had been accustomed to local self-government there. In 1669 they presented the governor with a petition of eleven grievances, the most important of which called for an Assembly.

The governor denied most of their requests but he did yield on several important points; he granted them the right to elect a constable and a Board of Overseers who, in turn, appointed the justices of the peace. Later, these rights were extended to other towns and villages in the colony.

Governor Nicholls returned to England and Colonel Francis Lovelace was sent over. He ruled from 1668 to 1674 and proved himself an able governor. One of his first acts was to establish friendly relations with the Indians. He bought Staten Island from them and the record states that he paid with "38 coats, 30 shirts, 30 kettles, 20 guns, 30 hoes and 50 knives." The Indians left and the Dutch who owned farms on Staten Island were able to buy more land.

Complaints came to the governor from the Indians living on the northern part of Manhattan; white men's cattle roamed all over their cornfields and ruined them, and more and more white men were moving into Indian hunting grounds. The Indians were paid and they moved from the island.

From time to time a high British official journeyed up the Hudson River to renew a peace treaty with the powerful Indian Five Nation Confederation. This was important as the French in Canada were always trying to turn them against the English. The loss of Indian loyalty would endanger the security of the frontier settlements and the loss of the Indian fur trade to the French would be a heavy blow to the economy. The gifts the Indians received kept them loyal to the English.

England and Holland had engaged in two wars in Europe and the Dutch in New York sympathized with the mother country. They thought that taxes here were too high and they were losing privileges to the English.

The third war between these countries involved New York. In August 1673, a Dutch convoy of twenty-one ships under the command of Admiral Cornelis Evertsen sailed into New York harbor and demanded its surrender. The fort was unable to resist because the guns had been spiked by Dutch sympathizers. Not a shot was fired and the city was taken by the Dutch. It was renamed New Orange. Governor Lovelace left for England and a new set of Dutch officials came to rule the colony.

The New Englanders on Long Island made demands on the Dutch: religious freedom; recognition of their Indian patents, that is, land grants; and most important of all, no taxation without representation.

They were still negotiating with the Dutch when in February 1674 the two European governments signed a peace treaty and the Dutch gave "New Orange" back to the English. The colony was renamed New York. Major Edmund Andros was sent to govern.

In 1681 the people demanded a voice in the levying of taxes and the right to make their own laws instead of those being made for them three thousand miles away in England. They wanted an Assembly. When the duke rejected their demands, New Yorkers refused to pay the customs duties.

The duke depended on New York for the money to support his extravagant way of living. When the money stopped

In 1674 the Dutch governor of "New Orange" relinquished control of the city to the English

coming, he gave in and sent Colonel Thomas Dongan with instructions to set up an election program for a General Assembly. The new governor (1683–88) announced that the first Assembly was to meet at Fort James in October 1683. Those who were eligible to vote chose eighteen delegates from all over the colony to represent them.

The Assembly was given the power to tax the people but the governor was to control the money. The Assembly adopted the "Charter of Liberties and Privileges," which provided for a regularly held Assembly composed of delegates elected by freeholders and freemen. A freeholder was someone who owned, free of debt, an estate valued at about forty pounds. Freemen were those who paid fees to the corporation of New York and were granted "freedomes" (a kind of work permit) to engage in their skilled occupation. The charter also included the right to freedom of worship and trial by jury.

The Duke of York approved the charter and the people were jubilant—they had won a real victory! Actually, the Assembly represented mainly the privileged class; it represented the people only in the sense that it protected the entire colony from too much interference and authority by the royal governor.

Governor Dongan knew that the rich merchants and the aristocratic landowners could be counted on as allies and he gave some of them manorial privileges. This meant that they could conduct their vast estates on the old English feudal system that England had long since discarded.

And favoring the rich merchants, he gave them certain monopolies (control), particularly that of the flour trade by passing the Bolting Act. (Bolting is sifting the outer hull of the grain which is then sifted into flour.) Also, he decreed that flour could be shipped only from New York City.

This enraged both upstate farmers and Long Island farmers who could bolt their own wheat and ship it from local wharves much cheaper. Besides, the increased cost was ruining their trade with Boston and the West Indies.

Word came from England that King Charles II had died and that the Duke of York was now King James II. New Yorkers rejoiced. It was James himself who had given them a charter of rights. But now the king had second thoughts about the charter and he withdrew it.

The people protested; they had enjoyed this first taste of self-government and would not willingly give it up.

The clamor over the loss of their rights was still heard when New Yorkers woke one morning in spring 1688 to find that they were no longer New Yorkers! With one stroke of the pen, King James had lumped them together with New

Jersey and the New England colonies into a dominion, to be ruled over by one governor.

The reason for it might have been acceptable had they been consulted in the matter. England had trouble with the French in Europe, and the French in Canada had been attacking New York settlements. Also, they were bribing the Indians with gifts so that they would give their loyalty and their fur trade to them instead of to the English.

The new governor of the Dominion of New England, Sir Edmund Andros, arrived in New York in 1688 and then went to Boston, leaving Francis Nicholson as acting governor. Andros's action in Boston alerted the New Yorkers to expect the worst; he abolished the Massachusetts Assembly and took away other rights from the people.

Then, in November, an event took place in England that gave the colonials new hope. The English had risen against King James and he had fled. His daughter Mary and her husband, William, Prince of Orange, were asked to come to rule England.

News of this reached Boston in March. The people threw Governor Andros into jail and brought the Assembly back.

Although King William III gave back the rights that James had taken away, the acting governor of New York, Nicholson, ignored this, and ruled with a council of three. New Yorkers, however, were determined to regain their rights and were discussing how to do this when Louis XIV of France declared war on England.

French Canadians and their Indian allies now swooped down on New York villages. Albany and Schenectady had cause for alarm, and now New York City was threatened from the sea as well as by land—a French fleet had been sighted sailing toward it.

Rumors cropped up everywhere; the French would forcibly convert everyone to Catholicism. Confusion and excitement mounted and threatened to paralyze the city.

Nicholson and his council of three proved incapable of handling the crisis.

The unrest grew worse and spread throughout the colony. Meetings were held and even the militia spoke out against this "government of tyrants." Now the rumors gave out that James, who had been converted to Catholicism, had fled to France and that the French king was sending troops to New York to seize it and put to the sword those who resisted conversion.

Riots broke out in Queens, in Suffolk, and Westchester. Soldiers refused to obey their officers; the people armed themselves and the acting governor and his officials did nothing to restore the rights of the people and thus halt the worsening situation.

The Leislerian Rebellion

One who spoke out against the government was Jacob Leisler, a wealthy wine merchant.

Not much is known of the early life of this man who dominated the scene during those two years of turmoil. He came to America in 1660 when he was twenty years old and was a soldier in the employ of the Dutch West India Company. Some people claimed that he was a German, others said that he was Dutch-born, while the Huguenots said that he was one of theirs. But no matter how doubtful his origin, this much is known with certainty—that he was called on to lead a revolt and that in his two years as acting governor he brought democracy for the first time into the lives of the ordinary people.

He was known to be a brave man, hot-tempered, and of strong views that clashed frequently with those of the governor and his council that consisted of aristocrats, Stephen van Cortland, Frederick Philipse, and Nicholas Bayard. But he was highly respected by many people. He had served

Citizens of New York signed a declaration urging Jacob Leisler to be the acting governor

as a justice of the peace, was captain of the militia, and deacon of the Dutch Reformed Church.

It was said that once, while on a business voyage to Europe, he was seized by Turkish pirates and held for ransom and that a purse was collected in New York for his release.

In May 1689, over four hundred citizens of New York signed a declaration urging him to be the acting governor. He agreed to serve, and led the militia to the fort, seized it, and took control of the city. That same day he wrote the "Humble Address of the Militia" to the king and queen, stating they were waiting for royal orders. Nicholson, un-

able to stem the tide of rebellion, returned to England and gave his account of the "Desperate and deplorable State of Government in New York."

Leisler dismissed the aristocratic members of the council, the corrupt officials, and customs men, and he replaced them with those loyal to him.

He was hailed as the "Champion of freedom." An Assembly was set up and the people of New York City had the right to vote for a mayor. This was the first and only time that this happened in colonial New York. The monopolies were abolished, the tax burden was more justly spread among the people and real self-government was introduced. Leisler urged the people to learn how to govern themselves by taking part in public affairs.

The merchants and landowners in Albany refused to recognize Leisler as acting governor. In 1690 the French and Indians burned Schenectady to the ground and captured those they had not killed. Albany was next in line of march. Leisler sent troops to defend the city and the people accepted his rule.

Again there were rumors of a French plot to seize New York and kill all Protestants. A Committee of Safety was organized and Leisler was elected as commander-in-chief. He believed that the French could be defeated if the colonies united on a plan for common defense. On May 1, 1690, he sent out a call for the first congress of American colonies to meet in New York to work on a plan to attack Canada.

Delegates of colonies in Massachusetts, Plymouth, and Connecticut met with the New Yorkers. Rhode Island and Maryland pledged their support. Although the plan did not get beyond the discussion stage, this meeting is of historic importance because, for the first time, the colonies met to plan a common defense. Unity of action meant protection for all, Leisler believed.

While the first colonial congress was being held, King William III appointed Colonel Henry Sloughter governor of New York and named Major Richard Ingoldsby lieutenant governor. And once again Philipse, van Cortland, and Bayard were appointed members of the council. This was a warning of danger to Leisler for earlier he had imprisoned Bayard.

Ingoldsby arrived in January 1691, and at once contacted the "natural allies of the king," the aristocrats and wealthy merchants. They considered Leisler a troublemaker who had incited the lower classes to rebel. Ingoldsby led his

A proclamation issued by Jacob Leisler on October 30, 1690

soldiers to the fort and ordered Leisler to surrender his command. Leisler refused; he would do so only if ordered by the king or the governor. Ingoldsby then billeted his troops in City Hall.

For two weeks he had the soldiers drilling and marching around the city. Ingoldsby gave orders and Leisler gave orders. The people were nervous over this new development. Leisler knew that divided authority divided and confused the people and he ordered Ingoldsby to dismiss his soldiers. He refused. Then Leisler ordered his men to shoot. Two soldiers were killed and several were wounded.

This caused great excitement—shooting the king's men was high treason! Opposition to Leisler began to rise.

Governor Sloughter arrived and ordered Ingoldsby to seize the fort. Leisler refused to surrender until the king's orders were presented. His enemies used these two acts as proof of treason to the crown and demanded that he be

An open clash between Leisler's men and Ingoldsby's troops resulted in the death of two British soldiers

brought to trial. Leisler and his son-in-law, Jacob Milborne, and their aides were arrested.

The aides were released, but a special court was set up to try Leisler and Milborne. When the judges were selected Leisler knew that he was doomed, for they were his known enemies. They found him guilty and sentenced him to death. Leisler appealed to the king but the governor was as much in a hurry to silence the leader of the rebellion as were the aristocrats. Without waiting for word from the king, he signed the death warrant and all of Leisler's property was seized.

As Leisler was about to be hanged, he made a statement that expressed his deep concern for the people he had led— he said that he hoped that all malice and hatred that had been aroused by the rebellion would die with him.

The effects of the Leisler Rebellion did not end with its leader's death. He had repealed many unjust laws and they were not restored. The Assembly was continued.

But the question, was Leisler right or wrong, continued to divide the colony. He had won the support of the mass of the people who, for the first time in American history, had risen against a tyranny. Important men saw these people as a check to the power of the aristocrats and the royal governor and two parties shaped up—the Leislerians, who believed in greater democracy, and the court party, which didn't.

The Leislerians won control of the Assembly in 1695 and repealed the Bolting monopoly as well as the penalties on Leisler's followers. They moved to clear the charge of treason against their dead leader, and four years after his execution, Parliament agreed to review his case. Leisler's name and his son-in-law's were cleared and their property restored to their family.

No one knows where Leisler is buried. A handsome monument was erected to him by the Huguenots in New Rochelle. He was one of the founders of this city where he owned land and helped the Huguenots settle there when they fled from persecutions in France.

Chapter 4:

Smugglers, Privateers, and Pirates

Like the other governors before him, Benjamin Fletcher
(1692–98) favored the aristocrats and the rich merchants,
as he had to rely on them to support his policies. He gave
them enormous grants of land for little money and expected
them to close their eyes to the corrupt way in which he was
amassing a fortune. It was no secret that he was receiving
huge sums from pirate captains who used New York for
trading and supply purposes. Nor was it a secret that he was
involved with some merchants in financing pirates. Many
colonial merchants thrived on smuggling, privateering, and
piracy, and Governor Fletcher's hands reached into their
pockets.

The colonies, through a new navigation act, were forced
to buy goods only from or through England. They resented
this control of trade and the high customs duties. Another
ruling they objected to was that all goods sent from or to
the colonies had to go on British ships.

Smuggling became a form of defiance.

Some merchants went in for smuggling and became rich. Although it was not as profitable as pirating or privateering, it had advantages; it was not as risky and did not involve murder on the high seas. The penalty for smuggling was high, but offenders were hard to catch as there were numerous approaches to the land and since customs officials were often bribed.

Privateering was actually legalized pirating. During those years governments at war commissioned the captains of commercial ships to capture those flying the flag of the enemy. Such ships were outfitted with guns. Ships and cargoes captured by a privateer were sold and the money was divided among the captain, the crew, officials, and members of the royal court. Respectable New York merchants and aristocratic landowners made fortunes by equipping ships to prowl the seas as privateers.

Pirates felt themselves welcome in New York. In dealing with the authorities, the pirate ships anchored at a point

Pirates came ashore with
pockets full of silver

near the eastern end of Long Island and several of the crew went to negotiate with the governor for permission to enter and for protection. The pirates came with pockets full of silver that they spent freely. Merchants welcomed them because they could buy oriental rugs, silks, ivories, and other rare items at a fraction of their original cost.

The capturing of ships, looting, and killing went on even when the governments were no longer at war with each other. This piracy was a great loss to merchants whose ships, cargoes, and sailors vanished with nothing but a burned hulk afloat to tell its sad tale. Finally, England decided to take action.

The man chosen to war on pirates and make the seas a safe passageway was a former English naval officer, Captain William Kidd.

Captain William Kidd

The son of a Scot clergyman, William Kidd settled in New York City in 1689 and became a businessman. He lived in a handsome, lavishly furnished home close to the harbor and was highly regarded in the community. A few years later he sailed to England on business. While there he met important officials and New York merchants who convinced him that he was the man to fight piracy. He was given the right to capture any French ship on the high seas (England and France were at war again), and so he was started in the privateering business. Among the shareholders of this company were King William, who was to receive 10 percent of all profits (some reports say 50 percent); the Earl of Oxford; Sir Edward Dressel, the first Lord of the Admiralty; Lord Bellomont, governor of New York; Frederick Philipse, lord of Philipse Manor of New York; and Robert Livingston, lord of Livingston Manor.

Articles of Agreement,

Made the 10th Day of *October*, in the Year of our Lord 1695. Between the Right Honourable *RICHARD* Earl of *BELLOMONT* of the one part, and *Robert Levingston* Esq;

AND

Captain William Kid,

Of the other part.

WHEREAS the said Capt. *William Kid* is desirous of obtaining a Commission as Captain of a Private Man of War in order to take Prizes from the King's Enemies, and otherways to annoy them; and whereas certain Persons did some time since depart from *New-England*, *Rode-Island*, *New-York*, and other parts in *America* and elsewhere, with an intention to become Pirates, and to commit Spoils and Depredations, against the Laws of Nations, in the *Red-Sea* or elsewhere, and to return with such Goods and Riches as they should get, to certain places by them agreed upon; of which said Persons and Places, the said Capt. *Kid* hath notice, and is desirous to fight with and subdue the said Pirates, as also other Pirates with whom the said Capt. *Kid* shall meet at Sea, in case he be impowered so to do; and whereas it is agreed between the said Parties, That for the purpose aforesaid a good and sufficient Ship, to the liking of the said Capt. *Kid*, shall be forthwith bought, whereof the said Capt. *Kid* is to have the Command. Now these Presents do witness, and it is agreed between the said Parties,

I. That the Earl of *Bellomont* doth covenant and agree, at his proper Charge, to procure from the King's Majesty, or from the Lords Commissioners of the Admiralty (as the Case shall require) one or more Commissions, impowering him the said Capt. *Kid* to act against the King's Enemies, and to take Prizes from them, as a private Man of War in the usual manner; and also to fight with, conquer and subdue Pirates, and to take them and their Goods; with other large and beneficial Powers and Clauses in such Commissions as may be most proper and effectual in such Cases.

II. The said Earl of *Bellomont* doth covenant and agree, That within three Months after the said Capt. *Kid's* departure from *England*, for the purposes in these Presents mentioned, he will procure, at his proper charge, a Grant from the King, to be made to some indifferent and trusty Person, of all such Mechandizes, Goods, Treasure and other things as shall be taken from the said Pirates, or any other Pirate whatsoever, by the said Capt. *Kid*, or by the said Ship, or any other Ship or Ships under his Command.

III. The said Earl doth agree to pay four Fifth parts, the whole in Five parts to be divided, of all Moneys which shall be laid out for the buying such good and sufficient Ship for the purposes aforesaid, together with Rigging and other Apparel and Furniture thereof, and providing the same with competent victualling the said Ship, to be approved of by the said Parties; and the said other one Fifth part of the said Charges of the said Ship to be paid for by the said *Robert Levingston* and *William Kid*.

IV. The said Earl doth agree, That in order to the speedy buying the said Ship, in part of the said four parts of Five of the said Charges, he will pay down the sum of sixteen hundred Pounds, by way of Advance, on or before the sixth day of *November* next ensuing.

V. The said *Robert Levingston* and *William Kid* do jointly and severally covenant and agree, That on and before the sixth day of *November*, when the said Earl of *Bellomont* is to pay the said Sum of sixteen hundred pounds as aforesaid, they will advance and pay down four hundred pounds in part of the Share and Proportion which they are to have in the said Ship.

VI. The said Earl doth agree, to pay such further Sums of Money as shall compleat and make up the said four parts of Five of the Charges of the said Ship's Arrival, Furniture and Victualling, unto the said *Robert Levingston* and *William Kid* within seven Weeks after the date of these Presents; and in like manner the said *Robert Levingston* and *William Kid* do agree to pay such further Sums as shall amount to a fifth part of the whole Charge of the said Ship within seven Weeks after the date of these Presents.

A   VII The

The first page of the contract authorizing Captain Kidd to fight piracy

Captain Kidd outfitted his frigate with thirty-four guns and a crew and set sail. He reached Madagascar, the traditional haunt of the pirates. The period that follows belongs more to fiction than to history, for nothing was heard from Captain Kidd for a long while. Sailors returning from voyages told stories that he had turned pirate.

The captain, it was said, sailed into the Indian Ocean where he captured a ship that carried great treasures, some of them intended for an important Mogul of India. This enraged the Mogul and he threatened to stop England's trade with India and China if the pirate was not caught and punished.

The king of England and important men had made great fortunes from trading with India and they did not intend to lose the source of these riches. They made a peace offering to the Mogul by ordering the arrest of Captain Kidd.

But Captain Kidd did not know this as he set sail for America. He must have known that stories of his pirating were being told by returning sailors, but he did not worry as he knew that Governor Bellomont and powerful people in New York were too involved in his ventures to take action against him.

In 1699 Captain Kidd landed on Gardiner's Island, at the eastern end of Long Island. It is believed that while his lawyer was in conference with the governor, Kidd buried his treasure.

Placed under arrest, he showed papers to prove he had taken only pirate ships or those of countries at war with England. (These papers mysteriously disappeared and were referred to but never produced at his trial.) He was sent to England where he was formally charged with piracy and the murder of one of his crew, William Moore, although it was known that the man had mutinied.

He stood trial for murder and piracy in Old Bailey Court

in London and was neither allowed to testify on his own behalf nor to hire his own lawyer. It is on record that he said, "I hope that I have not offended against the law, but if I have, it was the fault of others who knew better and made me the tool of their ambition and avarice, and who now think it to their interest that I should be removed out of the world." He was found guilty and hanged in Execution Dock on the shores of the Thames, May 23, 1701.

The important papers that had disappeared were later found, and even today it is still a puzzling question—was he a pirate or scapegoat for those who had great political power?

Many poems and songs were written about Captain Kidd, for whom there was great sympathy. One of the popular ones is:

> My name is Captain Kidd who has sailed,
>   who has sailed.
> My name is Captain Kidd who has sailed,
>   who has sailed.
> My name is Captain Kidd
>   what the laws did still forbid
> Unluckily I did, while I sail'd, while I sail'd.

And the final stanza:

> Take warning now by me, for I must
>   die, I must die.
> Take warning now by me, for I must die.
> Take warning now by me, and shun bad
>   company
> Lest you come to hell with me, for I
>   must die,
> Lest you come to hell with me, for I
>   must die.

Governors, Good and Bad

New York had more than its share of dishonest or incompetent governors. Rarely were they appointed because they were qualified for the important post but because they had powerful friends at the royal court. Most governors thought of the appointment as a means of getting rich and sometimes this was their main and only success while they held office.

Governor Fletcher was dismissed in 1697 when the Leislerians sent to the king reports of his corruption, listing the bribes he took when he gave away enormous tracts of lands, the bribes from pirate captains, and other misdeeds.

His successor, the Earl of Bellomont, proved as corrupt. He died while in office. Lieutenant Governor John Nanfan was sent temporarily until Lord Cornbury was appointed in 1702. Lord Cornbury promptly removed every Leislerian from office.

As a governor he was neither capable nor wise, and at times his outrageous social behavior shocked the upper class. But he was related to Queen Anne, and as such he brought a social glamor to the city.

He squandered the public money, and this, too, could be forgiven as New Yorkers were by now accustomed to governors who pocketed the public funds. But it was a time of depression, and the governor kept draining the treasury and mismanaging his high office. Even the aristocrats had enough of Lord Cornbury's outrageous behavior and were vastly relieved when he was recalled in 1708.

Now the Assembly managed to win complete control of the public money and how it was to be spent. Of course the governors fought to gain back this control, and they used their power by not calling for elections. Sometimes seven or more years passed without an election. New Yorkers fought this, and finally the governor had to approve a law requiring that elections be held every three years.

To some extent the Assembly stopped being the tool of the governors, for, in order to be elected, an assemblyman had to consider the wishes of those eligible to vote.

Then, for about twenty years, the colony was ruled by governors who were both competent and honest. Colonel John Montgomerie, who held the post from 1728 to 1731, was reasonable and honest. When he died, Rip van Dam, the head of the Council, took over his duties at full salary until William Cosby arrived in 1732 to assume the office of governor. And then the fierworks began.

Governor Cosby demanded that Rip van Dam refund half the salary he had earned in his thirteen months in office. This was refused. The governor then asked the Supreme Court, which the Assembly had created in 1691, to create a special court to consider the case. Chief Justice Lewis Morris, Sr. (whose position depended on the goodwill of the governor), attacked the constitutionality of this special court. The governor fired Morris.

For some years Lewis Morris, Sr., had been the leader of the more liberal faction of the Assembly. The backbone of his party were the small farmers, shopkeepers, and artisans. In the election of 1733 they swept him and his son into the Assembly.

Zenger Fights for Freedom of the Press

William Bradford began publishing the first newspaper in New York City in 1725. The *New York Gazette*, a weekly, carried reports of Assembly or Council meetings, the views of Governor Cosby and his supporters, and items of local interest. He soon became the official printer. Governor Cosby was always flattered and his policies were endorsed in this paper.

THE
New - York Weekly JOURNAL.

Containing the freſheſt Advices, Foreign, and Domeſtick.

MUNDAY January 27th, 1734.

Juſtum et tenaeem propoſiti Virum,
Non civium Ardor prava jubentium,
Non Vultus inſtantis Tyranni,
Mente quatit ſolida.

Hor.

HE firſt eſſential Ingre-
dient Neceſſary to
form a Patriot, is Im-
partiality; for if a
Perſon ſhall think
himſelf bound by
any other Rules but thoſe of his own
Reaſon and Judgment, or obliged to
follow the Dictates of others, who
ſhall appear the Heads of the Party
he is ingaged in, he ſinks below the
Dignity of a Humane Creature, and
voluntarily reſigns thoſe Guides which
Nature has given him, to direct him
in all Spheres of Life.

The Coldneſs, and ſometimes Diſ-
dain, which a Man governed thus by
the Principles of Honour generally
meets with on ſuch Occaſions from
the Friends he has ever acted in Con-
cert with, for the former Part of his
Life, are Conſiderations which but
too often ſubdue the beſt inclined Spirits, and prevail with them to be
paſſive and obedient, rather than ac-
tive and reſolute : But if ſuch Per-
ſons could but once feel the Comfort
and Pleaſure of having done their
Duty, they would meet with a ſuffi-
cient Reward within themſelves, to
over ballance the Loſs of their Friends,
or the Malice lof their Enemies.

Ambition and Avarice are two Vi-
ces, which are directly oppoſite to the
Character of a Patriot, for tho' an
Increaſe of Power, or of Riches, may
be the proper Reward of Honour and
Merit, and the moſt honeſt Stateſman
may, with Juſtice accept of either ;
yet when the Mind is infected with a
Thirſt after them, all Notions of
Truth, Principle and Independency
are Loſt in ſuch Minds, and, by
growing Slaves to their own Paſſions,
they become Naturally ſubſervient to
thoſe who can indulge and gratify
them.

In public Affairs it is the Duty of
every Man to be free from perſonal
Prejudices ; neither ought we to op-
poſe any Step that is taking for the
Good of our Country, purely becauſe
thoſe that are the Contrivers and Ad-
viſers of it, are Obnoxious to us.
There are but too many Precedents of
this Nature, when Men have caſt the
moſt black Colours on the Wiſeſt of
Adminiſtrations, becauſe thoſe that
had the Direction of Affairs were
their Enemies in private Life ; and
this ill Way of Judging may be attended with dangerous Conſequences to
the common Weal.

Intrepidity and Firmneſs are two
Virtues which every Patriot muſt be
Maſter of, or elſe all the other Talents
he is poſſeſs'd of are uſeleſs and barren.

Whoever, therefore, when he has
formed a Judgment on any Subject re-
lating

The January 27, 1734, issue of Peter Zenger's newspaper carried an article describing the characteristics of a patriot

His apprentice, John Peter Zenger, was a bright young man who, as he gained experience and knowledge, disagreed with Bradford's opinion of the governor; he thought Cosby greedy, corrupt, and bent on crushing the people's rights.

Backed by Lewis Morris and his followers, Zenger started The *New York Weekly Journal* in 1733. From the beginning he let it be the voice of the people. He frequently printed the program of political and economic reforms put forward by the Morris faction. The paper attacked Chief Justice James de Lancey and the governor in thinly disguised fables, in ballads, poems, and lampoons.

One day Zenger printed a "long, loud cry" against the Cosby administration. The governor acted promptly. Handbills were distributed on November 6, 1734, promising a reward of "twenty pounds for the person who knew the author of the Scandalous Songs or Ballads, highly defaming the Administration of his Majesty's Government in this province that appeared in John Peter Zenger's New York Weekly Journal."

The Council ordered the city hangman to make a bonfire of four issues of Zenger's paper. The mayor and the aldermen refused to permit this, but the sheriff's slave burned these papers. Zenger was arrested.

This caused a great stir in the city of ten thousand people. Although they were divided for or against Zenger, the jury was not. The twelve men who had been chosen to decide whether there was sufficient evidence to hold Zenger for trial decided in favor of the young publisher.

The governor was enraged, and now he had charges of seditious libel brought against Zenger. Libel means saying or printing that which will injure another, but *seditious* libel is much more serious because it means injuring or trying to destroy the government. This was treason.

Zenger and the people on his side had cause to be alarmed when the two most prominent lawyers in New York, James

A bonfire was made of four issues of Peter Zenger's newspaper

Alexander and William Smith, were disbarred by the chief justice for contempt. Both were known to be sympathetic to the defendant. This meant that the publisher would be left without the defense of an able lawyer. Lewis Morris sought help outside New York.

In August 1735, Zenger was brought to trial. It was held in City Hall, and people jammed the courtroom while a huge crowd waited outside. A jury was chosen. The first to speak was the lawyer for the governor's side who, he said, was speaking on behalf of *His Majesty's* government. To criticize the king was treason; therefore Zenger should be hanged.

The case for the defense seemed lost. Just then an old man rose from the crowd of spectators to speak for Zenger. The governor's supporters and all the aristocrats present were stunned—the old man was Andrew Hamilton, the most famous lawyer in all the colonies.

Zenger's backers had secretly arranged for him to appear

so dramatically, and the lawyer had consented, for Zenger and freedom of the press had become a burning issue in all the colonies. Now the two sides shaped up for the historic battle.

The arguments focused on the main question the jury was to decide. The chief justice said that the main question was whether Zenger was guilty of libel or not. Hamilton disagreed. He said that the question was whether the statements printed by Zenger were true or not, and that if they were true, he was not guilty.

Then he went on to prove the truth of Zenger's statements: that judges had been removed by the governor without cause, that new courts had been started without the consent of the Assembly, and that some men in the colony were denied their votes, although they were eligible to vote.

Proving that all this had actually happened, Hamilton went on to say that if a man were punished for printing the truth, it meant the end of all liberty for the people. His speech to the jury was simple but forceful and its keynote was liberty. He said that if officials oppressed the people and then punished them for complaining, there would be an end to liberty and that not only was Zenger on trial, but all publishers in every colony.

Finally, he pleaded with the jury to preserve liberty by admitting the right of a person to speak and write the truth, because if Zenger lost, the freedom of the press would be lost to all.

. . . the question before the court, and you, gentlemen of the jury, is not of small nor private concern; it is not the cause of a poor printer, nor of New York alone, which we are now trying. No! It may in its consequence affect every freeman that lives under a British government on the main of America. It is the best cause. It is the cause of liberty! . . .

Andrew Hamilton left the courtroom in triumph following Zenger's trial

The jury decided that Zenger had printed only the truth and set him free. The people in the courtroom cheered and stamped their feet to applaud the verdict. Those outside roared out their approval.

Hamilton refused a fee, saying that "the preservation of the freedom of the press was payment enough."

A grand banquet and ball was given in his honor and the mayor presented him with a gold box containing a scroll that gave him the freedom of the city. He was greeted everywhere as a hero, and crowds followed him with banners when he took the ferry for the first lap of his long journey by sea and land to Philadelphia. The gun at the Battery fired off a salute to him.

In this trial not only was the freedom of the press established but also the principle that the people had the right to criticize and protest against the acts of those in power.

Chapter 5:

Immigrants All

New York colony did not keep pace in population growth with the other colonies because immigrants found it difficult to buy farming land. Much of the land in upper New York was owned by eleven families who preferred to rent rather than sell. Also, the colony grew slowly because the Iroquois were not friendly to those moving into their hunting grounds. And there was always the fear of attack by the Canadian French and their Indian allies.

Gradually, as trading posts were set up in the northern and western parts of New York, small settlements sprang up. In 1678 a group of twelve French families settled New Paltz in the Wallkill Valley. After 1700 the Dutch trading post at Schenectady was increased by some English families.

Then, in 1710, the largest single national group arrived. It consisted of about twenty-five hundred Germans from the Palatinate, a district along the Rhine. They had fled to

England when the armies of the French king, Louis XIV, invaded their land and drove them out. The English government sent them in ten ships to New York where they were to settle and work at making tar and cutting down trees to make masts for the Royal Navy.

A camp was set up for them along the Hudson River near the site of present-day Germantown and West Camp, but the Germans were dissatisfied with the conditions. Before long they abandoned the camp and about one hundred families went to the Schoharie Valley, which had been promised them. They had already built seven little villages when land speculators from Albany claimed the land and the Germans had to buy or leave. Some bought while the rest went on to Pennsylvania where land was cheap.

High taxes and persecution were sending Scottish and Irish families to the New World. They settled in the Mohawk Valley. Most of the people who settled in America came to escape religious or political oppression—and ofttimes both.

A pioneer had to be brave as well as strong to make a life for his family on the frontier. First, he had to make a clearing in this raw wilderness, chop down trees, remove rocks and thick, tough underbrush before he could build a cabin. Then he had to plow the hard virgin soil and plant. If he was wise he made friends with the Indians, learned from them how to plant corn which was eaten by man and animals and which became the most popular crop. The pioneers learned from the Indians how to hunt and this provided meat and clothing for their families.

Each pioneer home was like a small producing plant. The women spun flax or wool shearings from sheep into thread to weave cloth for clothing. They preserved beef and pork in salt which provided income as well as food, since any that was not needed by the family was sold to a merchant who exported it. The pioneer made his own furniture. The

Pioneer women made soft soap by leaching water through potash to make lye, which was then boiled with grease

forest was his wealth, for besides providing shelter and fuel, profitable use was made of the ashes of the trees that had been chopped down and burned. This was potash, a good cash item, for it was needed as fertilizer and in the making of soap and bleaching of cloth. With this cash pioneer families bought what could not be made in the home—farming tools, tea, salt, muskets, and so forth.

In New York City there was always work for an immigrant, particularly if he had a skill. Cabinet-makers, coopers, and chandlers were in great demand, as well as wig-makers whose fancy creations sat on the heads of the moneyed people. Newcomers were also in demand as bakers, cobblers, bricklayers, cordwainers, blacksmiths, shipbuilders, and brewers.

Social Classes—the Right To Vote

Social classes began to develop early in New York. At the top were the great landowners and wealthy merchants who brought with them the ways of life of the English aristocracy. Just below them were the leading professional men such as clergymen, lawyers, and high officials.

The middle class consisted of landowning farmers, shopkeepers, skilled craftsmen, and tavern keepers. Then there were the tenant-farmers, workers, soldiers, and shop clerks; apprentices who served a master for about seven years and who, provided with food and shelter, were taught a trade; indentured servants who worked for a period of years in exchange for their passage to America; and Negro slaves who worked as house servants or field hands on the large estates. The descendants of a small number of slaves brought by the Dutch had earned their freedom and worked on the docks or at various odd jobs. Some owned farms.

Harsh treatment by their owners made some slaves rebel in 1712. In 1741 nearly two hundred Negroes were arrested and charged with conspiracy to burn down New York City. It was the most unfair trial in colonial history. Many New Yorkers were so ashamed of this episode that reformers, led by Quakers, started a movement for better treatment for Negroes and removal of the harsh laws that were passed after the first uprising. They provided schooling for a number of Negro children. Some Negro slaves were skilled craftsmen. They bought their freedom and then opened their own shops. (The practice of slavery continued until 1826 when it was legally abolished in New York.)

Not all the population had the right to vote. Freemen and freeholders had to pay for the privilege. A freeholder whose estate was worth less than forty pounds or who was in debt, leasehold tenants, or those who worked for others (mostly the unskilled), and women and Negroes did not have the right to vote. By 1750 Negroes who met property qualifications were qualified to vote.

As the population increased, the various religious groups won the right to build their own churches. The Quakers who, under Dutch rule, were persecuted and could not have their own house of worship, had since built several meetinghouses on Long Island and in Westchester, while the community of four hundred Jews had, by 1695, erected a synagogue on Mill Street in New York City.

There were few Roman Catholics in New York before the Revolution, but several Jesuit missionaries from Canada worked among the Indians. Governor Dongan, an Irish Catholic, had built a small Catholic church, St. Peter's, and this took great courage for there was deep prejudice against them in the colonies. In 1700 there was a law condemning to death any priest caught in New York colony.

Education and Laws of Behavior

Most of the schools were founded by religious groups and were attended by less than half the children of the colony. In the northern and western parts of New York an even smaller number attended. Some of the frontier settlements had no schools in their early years.

The majority of students in the city schools did not continue their education beyond elementary school. Those whose parents could afford the cost engaged tutors or sent their sons to one of the few secondary schools that existed then. A small number of them went on to Yale, Harvard, or Princeton. King's College, now Columbia University, was founded in 1754. The first classes were held in a schoolhouse that belonged to Trinity Church. A little later enough money was raised, mainly through lotteries, for buildings, including a library. The first graduating class in June 1759 consisted of eight men.

Girls received their education at home or in a Dames' school, and wealthy parents engaged tutors to teach their daughters good manners, dancing, and foreign languages, usually French. Girls were not admitted to college.

The first graduating class of King's College (now Columbia University) consisted of eight men

The poor were not required to pay for the education of their children in church schools. Orphans and children of paupers were bound out as apprentices or servants.

Today grade-school teachers must be college graduates and many of them have higher degrees in education. But in the early colonial years teaching requirements were much less strict. The educated men preferred to do more profitable work. Then, too, the church-school teachers had to assist the minister in his duties.

Classes were held through most of the day and discipline was harsh. From diaries and stories of those days we read of the severe punishments for the least bit of inattention.

The Dutch language continued to be used in schools, particularly those in and near Albany, for years after New York had become an English colony. When more English teachers arrived and a serious effort was made to introduce the language into the schools, one schoolmaster was singled out for his particular success in achieving this in a short time. He did this by giving a metal piece each day to the first pupil who used a Dutch word. That pupil then turned the token over to the next person who spoke Dutch. The token was passed from pupil to pupil and when the school day ended the one who held the token was soundly whipped.

There were few printed books in colonial schools. Schoolmasters made "sum-books" by hand, and pupils copied the sums and rules into the small blank notebooks that they had made. The teacher made ink from a solid block of ink mixed with water. He had to write out copy for each subject which the pupils copied and learned.

Colonial children were not pampered and obedience to parents, their elders, teachers, and ministers was the required and usual behavior. The laws about this were very strict. One such law in Albany was:

> If any children be caught on the street playing, racing and shouting previous to the termination of the last preachment, the officers of justice may take the hat and upper garment, which shall not be restored to the parents until they have paid a fine of two guilders.

This, of course, meant punishment on arriving home, and as the sermons were very lengthy, you can see that Sunday was not a fun time for colonial children.

While the pillory, the cage, and the ducking stool were not used for children, those under fifteen years of age did not escape punishment. The youth who swore or used bad language was fastened to a stake in front of the City Hall with a bridle in his mouth and a bundle of rods tied under each arm and a poster on his chest telling exactly what he had done. A thief who stole cabbages from his neighbor stood for several days in the pillory with cabbages on his head so that "the punishment might fit the crime." The city whipper, according to an advertisement for one in 1751, was paid twenty pounds annually.

Even during the revolutionary period a cage stood in City Hall park in which to confine boys who profaned the Sabbath.

New York Takes On a New Look

The English put their mark on the city with more than their laws and their language. (By 1760 the majority of the population of thirteen thousand were of English stock.) No longer did the Dutch houses with steep sloping roofs and high front stoops dominate the scene. Now many were of English-style architecture—tall, square-shaped houses of two or three stories topped with balustrades and with brick chimneys at both ends. Some were of red brick trimmed with marble and some of yellow and red brick with a red-tiled roof.

By 1700, when the city had a population of four thousand, there were no longer any empty building lots along the waterfront. The streets there were cluttered with warehouses of all kinds, markets, crafts shops, and the auction shed where Negroes were sold and indentured servants auctioned off. Facing them were the oldest houses in town —the Dutch.

Nor were there empty spaces from the Battery to the Fields where the soldiers' barracks stood. Houses lined the streets along the half-mile cow path called Broadway, part of which was paved with cobblestones. The path ran a crooked line from the fort to Wall Street where Stuyvesant's wall had once kept out wolves, panthers, and other undesirables. Broadway was fast becoming the main road leading to the northern farms and forests and the village of Harlem.

Wolves still roamed the forest north of Wall Street, raiding farms and killing livestock. Farmers went in groups to hunt them and offered rewards for the pelts.

The first public library of the colony was housed in

Slaves were sold and indentured servants auctioned off in the auction shed on the waterfront in New York

the new City Hall. A jail was in another part of the building where criminals and those who owed money were kept until their debts were paid. Across the street stood the pillory, the stocks, and the whipping post. To the east and the west stood the homes of the workers and beyond them, along the rivers, were the fine estates of the wealthy. The more daring ones were beginning to build far north of the city—Greenwich Village.

On nights when there was no moon lanterns were hung outside every seventh house and the owners of the other six paid for the whale oil.

Bowling Green was a parade ground for soldiers and public meetings were held here, as were maypole dances and fairs.

A walk on the city streets was an adventure in sight, sound, and smell, for the street cleaning was left to the one thousand-odd hogs. By 1701 public street cleaning was a regular feature and on Friday the hausfrau swept all the house dirt into a heap in front of the house for the public cartmen who carried it away. People were fined for any dirt that accumulated outside their houses, but despite the law and as late as the Revolution, visitors wrote about the hogs having the run of the city and the heaps of refuse everywhere.

Taverns and inns served not only food and drink but also as a sort of commercial parlor where merchants, lawyers, and others enjoyed a few social hours and conducted their business.

A sign in one of these inns reveals not only the prices charged, but the practices of the times:

Four pence a night for Bed
Six pence with Supper.
No more than five to sleep in one bed.
No boots to be worn in bed.

The "Rattle Watch" patrolled the streets at night, swinging their rattles and calling out the hour and the weather. In 1734 every able-bodied citizen took his turn at standing watch about once a month. It was not until 1762 that a paid and standing police force took over the duties of patrol.

The citizens who patrolled the streets of colonial New York carried wooden rattles

The Postrider

The first regular mail from New York to Boston started on January 22, 1673. Until then Indian postriders, whose endurance and honesty people had to vouch for, carried the winter mail to Albany. In the summer the sloops that plied the Hudson carried mail to Albany and mail took from two to three weeks to reach the receiver.

The postrider to Boston took an old Indian trail along the easterly part of Manhattan to Harlem where he crossed the Harlem River by ferry. From there the trail led north to another ferry that crossed Spuyten Duyvil Creek to the mainland. This route became known as the Boston Post Road.

As the postrider rode into the deep wilderness of the Bronx and farther north, he marked his way by cutting notches into the bark of the trees. He changed horses at Hartford, Connecticut, and after leaving mail at the inn, he galloped on. He was told to keep a sharp eye for "fugitive soldiers and servants" who were probably on leave without permission.

The postrider was required to act "seemly in all things, to comport himself truly and soberly." He was ordered not to make a longer stay anywhere than "necessarily belongs to refreshing himself and his horse" and to "behave as a good postmaster ought to do."

He slept in farm houses along the way or, if the farms were too far apart, spent the night by his own campfire. He returned to New York a month later with letters from Boston. The mail was brought to the "coffee-house" and put on a table, where letters were thumbed over and studied by the public at large until the people to whom they were addressed claimed them.

A locked box stood in the office of the colonial secretary where out-going mail was collected.

As the population increased, weekly stage coaches plied between New York and various colonial cities. In 1741 the royal mail coach carrying passengers as well as mail was started to Long Island and then to Staten Island, New Jersey, on to Philadelphia, and then south. A few years later the stage coach began the trip to Boston twice every week.

Chapter 6:

The French and English Wars in America

From 1689 to 1748 the French and the English waged three wars in Europe and in America. The fourth and decisive struggle, known as the French and Indian War, lasted from 1754 to 1763. An English victory drove the French from most of American territory, leaving them only Louisiana.

If France had won this war you might now be reading this book in French, and it would be a different story indeed.

Both France and England wanted control of the fur trade and the water routes to Canada as well as the French-claimed lands in the western part of America.

New York's position on the Hudson-Mohawk rivers and Lake Champlain made the colony the key point in the struggles. Then, too, New York harbor was ice-free in winter and the French needed an ice-free harbor because in the winter it was not possible to reach Montreal and Quebec from her forts along the Ohio and Mississippi rivers. Whoever controlled these water routes controlled the interior lands and the rich fur trade. France ventured a fourth try to gain all this.

The Indians played an important part in these wars; the English and the French courted them as allies.

From the beginning of their settlement in Canada, the French succeeded in establishing friendly relations with the Canadian Indians as well as with those on the Great Lakes. A few Frenchmen went to live in Indian villages, learned their language, their customs, and helped them in their wars on New York Indians. The French built forts on the banks of Lake Erie and at Niagara, and the Indians traded their furs there in exchange for muskets, powder, steel traps, trinkets, and other things.

The Iroquois Indians lived in the central part of New York. They were a proud and warlike people and their leaders were very shrewd. They knew that the French and the English wanted them as allies and the advantages of playing off one against the other; they gave their loyalty to those from whom they had the most to gain. While they were inclined to favor the English because of their friendship with several Englishmen, they also respected the side that won battles, and the English had already lost three campaigns against the French.

The English learned that if they were to win a lasting victory over the French they would have to win and keep the friendship of the Indians. They chose William Johnson, who had great influence with the Iroquois, to be Superintendent of Indian affairs. His success in maintaining friendly relations with the Indians helped gain a few victories in the third French and English war, for which he was knighted.

An Irishman Pioneers the Northwest

William Johnson was only twenty-three years old when he set out to pioneer the northwestern part of New York. He was a nephew of Peter Warren, one of New York City's wealthiest men, who owned miles of land along the Mohawk River.

The idea of carving a town out of the forest appealed to the young Irishman, and taking a group of settlers among whom were a few skilled workmen, he sailed up the Hudson to Albany. There he hired wagons to carry his people and his supplies on the forty-mile ride through dense, unbroken woods.

Reaching his destination, near what is now Amsterdam, he saw to the building of the first few cabins and then he set out to visit the Mohawks. He won their friendship, learned their language, traditions, their games, and wore the Indian garb. He was adopted into the Iroquois Nation and given the name of Waraghiyaghey, which means chief director of affairs.

Johnson's friendship with the Indians paid off well. He set up a trading post and within five years made a fortune by trading furs for the goods that his uncle supplied. The Indians brought their furs to him because he treated them as his equals and did not cheat them.

He kept buying land, built more houses, erected a saw-mill, a flour mill, and several public buildings. As more people came to settle in the area, he convinced them of the importance of treating the Indians fairly and respecting them.

So great was Johnson's influence that during the third war between the French and the English in 1744 only he kept the Iroquois from going over to the French. For this service the British government made him a member of the Council of New York. When the French and Indian War broke out in 1754, Johnson was appointed Superintendent of Indian Affairs. The British suffered defeats in the first battles; Johnson won an early victory when, at the head of colonists and Indians he defeated the French force near Lake George. He was made a baronet.

Meanwhile, Sir William kept adding to his great estate (he then owned nearly half a million acres in the northwestern part of New York), and it was said that he got some one hundred thousand acres of this through dreams that he and an Indian chief had.

This chief was fond of colorful clothing and Johnson had a gaily embroidered scarlet silk coat. The chief told Johnson that in a dream he had been made a present of that coat. Sir William handed it over to him.

Several days later Sir William told the chief that he, too, had a dream; the Indian and his Council had made him a present of a tract of land of some one hundred thousand acres and so real was this dream that he was even able to draw a map showing its exact boundaries. The old chief paid a high price indeed for the scarlet silk coat.

The largest English trading post was at Oswego with its 150 Indian traders. It was the most important center for trade with the Indians as Niagara was for the French. Through the years the Indians kept bringing their furs to Johnson and buying their supplies from his store. The French looked with envious glances at this beehive of wealth. Rivalry for the fur trade was becoming sharper then in the 1750s and a fight for its control was rapidly shaping up.

In times of peace there was considerable trading between Albany and Montreal. In war it was the route of invasion to either Canada or New York, because of the Hudson and Mohawk rivers and the routes to Lake Champlain, which were the waterways to the interior of America. Thus Albany was strategically situated and important militarily. If the

French took it, the war would soon be on the doorsteps of New York City.

Unlike the English who made settlements, the French kept building forts to claim the land for France. They went deeper into the American lands by building a chain of forts below Lake Erie and in western Pennsylvania. They built a few more along the Allegheny and these protected their route to the Ohio River. Some of these forts were too close to the Virginia Colony for colonial comfort. The French and their Indian allies burned isolated cabins, killed the adults, and carried off the children.

This did not go unchallenged. In 1753 a group of Virginians led by George Washington went to fight the French in western Pennsylvania. A year later the fourth and final war between the French and the English broke out.

The Iroquois Are a Sometime Ally

A few northern settlements in New York had been attacked and the colony was now in greater danger than before because they no longer had the friendship of the Iroquois Confederation.

The Indians were cool to them because the English had destroyed their fort at Saratoga in 1747 and withdrawn from the area, thus leaving them exposed to the French and their allies. Then, too, speculators (those who buy to sell for profit) were cheating them out of their hunting grounds. Another grievance was that the New York Assembly had failed to vote a sum for the usual and expected gifts. William Johnson was no longer in charge of Indian Affairs and they grumbled about this.

The English government sent two regiments under the command of General Edward Braddock to fight the French. The colonials were expected to provide two more. The colonies decided to hold a conference in Albany on June

*The Indian chief
Tiyanoga was also known
as Hendrick*

19, 1754, to determine on a course of action. William
Johnson was influential in getting the Indian chiefs to
meet with the colonial leaders.

At this conference the Indians spoke their grievances.
The most outspoken chief, Hendrick, boldly put the blame
for English defeats on the English themselves:

> . . . 'tis your fault, brethren, that we are not strengthened
> by conquest, for we would have gone and taken Crown
> Point, but you hindered us. Instead of this you burnt your
> own fort at Saratoga which was a shame and a scandal to
> you. Look about your country and see, you have no forti-
> fications about you, and not even to this city, 'tis but a
> step from Canada and the French may easily come and
> turn you out of doors. Look about you and see all these
> houses full of beaver, and the money all gone to Canada.
> Likewise powder, lead and guns which the French make
> use of at Ohio. Look at the French, they are men, they are
> fortifying everywhere, but we are ashamed to say it, you
> are like women. . .

Other Indians complained that the English did not always play fair with them and neglected them while the French were always helpful. Another Indian urged that fair trading rules be put into practice and that Sir William be returned to the office in charge of Indian affairs.

Still another complained of the land speculators, and an Oneida sachem said to Johnson as he pointed to a speculator:

> You promised that you would keep this fire place clean from all filth and that no snake should come into this Council Room. That man sitting there . . . is a Devil and has stolen our land, he takes Indians slyly by the blanket one at a time and when they are drunk, puts some money in their bosoms, and persuades them to sign deeds . . .

At this conference Benjamin Franklin offered a plan for colonial unity so that their combined military forces could defeat the French. The plan he put forward later laid the basis for the unity that brought American independence.

As before, William Johnson persuaded the Iroquois to remain loyal. The New York Assembly gave the Indians thirty wagons of gifts and promises of cooperation were made.

The French and Indian War

At this Albany conference the colonial leaders agreed to furnish two regiments. General Braddock was to lead his English soldiers and the Virginia Provincial Militia against the French at Fort Duquesne in western Pennsylvania: General William Shirley, governor of Massachusetts, was to move north in an attack on Fort Niagara, and William Johnson was to command the army that would take Crown Point.

But the plans fell short of their objectives. The English were not used to long marches through dense forests and swamps. General Braddock, who had no experience fighting Indians, ignored the advice of colonials who had; they tried to warn him that the French and Indians always attacked from behind trees and that his soldiers' red coats made effective targets. He ignored their advice, rejected their tactics, and was badly beaten by the French and Indians.

The plans for attacking the forts at Niagara and Crown Point fell into enemy hands. General Shirley could not attack Fort Niagara because General Braddock, who was to have joined him, had been killed and his army was in retreat.

The Indians who had promised their help to the English again saw that the French were better fighters and ceased being hostile to them, as their hunting grounds were now exposed to them. This, of course, General Shirley did not know as he moved his army up the Mohawk Valley and counted on their support.

Johnson, who was to advance on Crown Point, was having a difficult time in Albany getting the needed supplies, wagons, and boats. His army consisted of New Yorkers, New Englanders, and fifty Mohawks under their chief Hendrick. They built Fort Edward before setting out for Crown Point.

The French commander at Crown Point decided not to wait for an attack. He moved south to Fort Edward so that he could take it and thus break Johnson's line of supply and force him to surrender. Indian scouts brought word to Johnson that the French were at Fort Edward and he sent a party to defend it. It was headed by the Indian chief Hendrick, who was killed when the French ambushed his men.

The French commander then attacked Johnson's troops

but he was forced back and lost many men. Johnson fought bravely and was wounded, but his men held the camp they had fortified and which is now known as Fort William Henry. The French suffered their first setback there, and they retreated to Carillon (Fort Ticonderoga).

Thus far the war seemed to be mainly French victories and all their trails of conquest led south to Oswego. Their main army was under the command Marquis de Montcalm. He seized Oswego and returned to Montreal with sixteen hundred prisoners and all the supplies his men and the wagons could carry.

Then he turned south to capture Fort William Henry. This gave him control of Lake George. And so went the war, with the French and Indians swooping down on forts and on settlements, killing and capturing the inhabitants

An old print depicted the two battles of Lake George

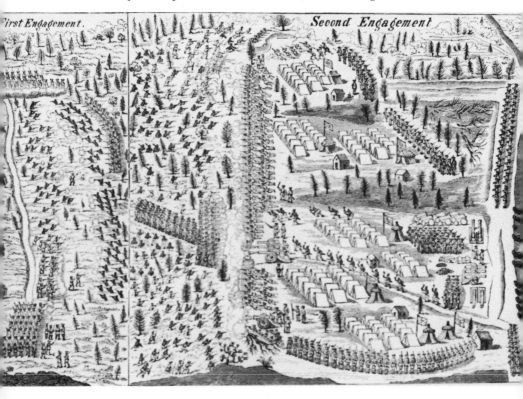

and advancing until they were in control of all northern and western New York.

There were still more defeats to come for the English. The army had lost many men and much equipment; the Mohawks were the only Indians who could be relied on and this was because of their loyalty to William Johnson.

At this time William Pitt became the chief minister in the English government and he decided that the war must be supported more effectively. The Royal Navy was ordered to cut off French supplies to America, more British troops were sent, and the colonials put more soldiers into the field.

The combined efforts resulted in the first English victory, but this did not happen until they had suffered a few defeats. General James Abercrombie, with fifteen thousand English and colonial soldiers, set out to take Fort Ticonderoga from General Montcalm. At the head of the army was young Lord Howe who understood the Indian way of fighting, and Major Israel Putnam with his two hundred Rangers. Putnam, who was later to command an army in the Revolutionary War, marched his Rangers through the wilderness but the English troops, unaccustomed to the dense woods, were slowed down. Then a challenge in French was called out. Shots were exchanged and Lord Howe fell. The Rangers fought bravely until the English and colonial troops reached them. The French tried to withdraw, and while some managed to escape, the rest were killed or captured.

The army pressed on to Fort Ticonderoga. Montcalm, who had received word of the defeat of his detachment, set his men to work cutting down trees and making a palisade around the fort.

Reaching Ticonderoga, Abercrombie ordered his men to attack. They were out in the open and exposed, while the French fired from behind the shelter of the stout walls.

The combined forces of the Indians and the English forced the French to withdraw from Crown Point

The British attacked six times that afternoon and retreated when night fell. It was a great victory for the French; not only had they defeated an army four times the size of their own, but they were still in possession of the strategic fort.

After news of Abercrombie's defeat, the colonial leaders took a greater hand in planning the campaign, and they concentrated their attacks on the French in the west. With a force of three thousand, one-third of whom were New Yorkers, they won Fort Frontenac on Lake Ontario and captured its supplies. This was a great loss to the French, since the fort was a shipping point between Montreal and Niagara, a direct line of supplies and communication. They were forced to retreat to La Presentation, now Ogdensburg, and then had to yield Fort Duquesne.

Now the war turned in England's favor, and the Iroquois became friendlier. General Wolfe was sent to capture Quebec. The French began to feel the impact of his brilliant leadership and were forced to withdraw from Crown Point and Fort Ticonderoga. General Wolfe took Quebec.

William Johnson and several hundred Indians moved to aid General John Prideaux in seizing Fort Niagara. The general was killed and Johnson became the commander. He recaptured Oswego and from then on the road to victory was all theirs.

With peace declared, Britain gained control of Canada and all the land of the French east of the Mississippi with the exception of Louisiana. Victory assured New Yorkers that the fur trade would continue to be a source of wealth. But more important, they could now make settlements in the northern and western part of the colony without fear of a French and Indian attack.

Chapter 7:

Taxes Cause Trouble

Victory, after the long war, gave England many problems. Now that Canada belonged to her and the American territory had been extended to the Mississippi, a standing army of about ten thousand would be required to guard the northern and western borders. Parliament decided to tax Americans to pay for part of this expense, and in 1764 passed the Sugar Act, which was a tax on all sugar imports. This new act prohibited, among other items the importation of all rum except that of British make and levied taxes on products bought from the Spanish or the French West Indies.

At the same time England sent more customs officials to America and set up more courts to enforce the Navigation Acts that some New Yorkers had for years ignored by smuggling or bribing customs officials.

Naval ships began patrolling the coast, stopping all merchant vessels in their path to inspect them. Shipowners and captains were closely watched; rewards were offered to informers and those who helped to catch smugglers shared in the sale of the cargo. The courts were kept busy.

Americans thought that the Sugar Act had been passed to help pay England's war debts and felt it was unjust. They, too, had suffered great loss in lives and the destruction of settlements. And they had provided soldiers to fight the French. They thought that England had no right to tax them except for the purpose of controlling its trade. England claimed the right to tax them for any purpose.

The Billeting Act, or Quartering Act, was one of the provisions of the Mutiny Act passed in 1765, which made the colonies provide barracks, bedding, and fuel for ten thousand soldiers. It provoked more resentment among New Yorkers than with other colonials because the city was the British military and administrative headquarters for all the colonies and so bore the heaviest burden. They felt they had given a good account of themselves fighting the French and were confident that they could now defend themselves; they did not want a standing army.

But the main thrust of colonial anger was against the Sugar Act. Petitions went in batches across the ocean; New York merchants appealed to the Board of Trade in London and the New York Assembly wrote to the king, to the House of Lords, to the Commons. Respectfully, but very definitely, they denied the right of Parliament to tax the peoples of the colony. They stated that if the British government taxed the colony without its consent, it would destroy the liberty and security of its people; that New York was loyal to Great Britain and that the Sugar Act would destroy colonial trade.

Then, to prove the seriousness of their protests, the New York Assembly ordered its Committee of Correspondence

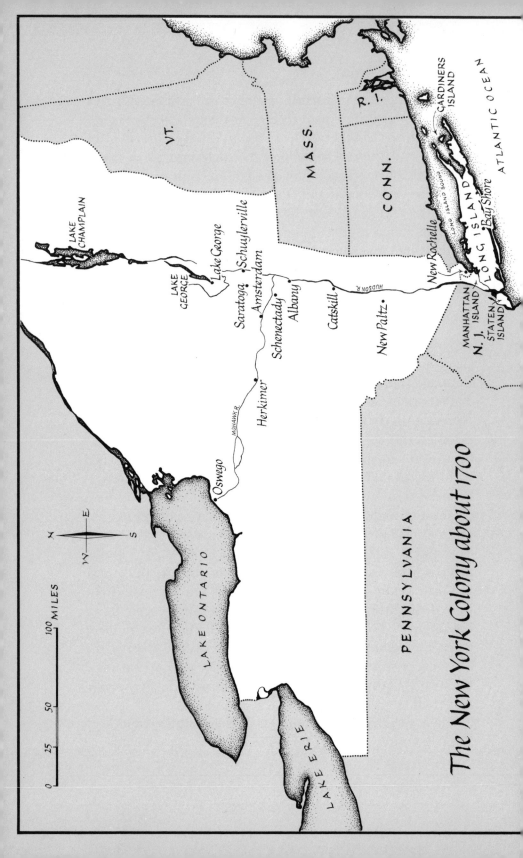

The New York Colony about 1700

ATLANTIC OCEAN

GARDINERS ISLAND

R. I.

MASS.

CONN.

VT.

LAKE CHAMPLAIN

LAKE GEORGE
Lake George

Saratoga • Schuylerville
Amsterdam

Schenectady
Albany

Catskill •

New Paltz •

HUDSON R.

New Rochelle

LONG ISLAND
Bay Shore

LONG ISLAND SOUND

MANHATTAN
N. J. ISLAND
STATEN ISLAND

Herkimer •

MOHAWK R.

Oswego •

LAKE ONTARIO

LAKE ERIE

PENNSYLVANIA

N
W   E
S

MILES
100   50   25   0

to write to all the colonies requesting their cooperation on a plan to fight this unfair tax.

Because of the Sugar Act, trade with the French and the Spanish West Indies fell off sharply and exports such as meat, lumber, wheat, and other products glutted the New York warehouses. Unemployment set in. Merchants suggested that the people stop importing British goods and begin manufacturing the things needed in the colony so that they would not have to rely on the mother country for them.

The British took the petitions lightly, ignored reports that the colonies were in a defiant mood, and in March 1765 took another step on the road to war. Parliament passed the Stamp Act.

This act required stamps to be bought and put on all newspapers, licenses, handbills, playing cards, dice, wills, deeds, and all legal documents.

The total disregard of their earlier petitions angered New Yorkers and now they sent petitions that hinted a threat: inasmuch as they had no representation in the Parliament that body had no right to tax them!

If Parliament had listened to the ground-swell of anger that surged up everywhere in the colonies, it would not have taken the next step. Not only were more soldiers to be sent to America to see that the new taxes were paid, but the Quartering Act now forced Americans to house and feed these soldiers. In other words, the colonials were to pay taxes they did not want to pay and were now required to support soldiers in their own homes who saw to it that they did pay.

Defiance was in the air, and for the first time a cry for independence was heard. An article printed in the *New York Gazette* on June 6, 1765, stated:

If the Welfare of the Mother Country necessarily requires a Sacrifice of the most natural rights of the Colonies, their

Right of making their own laws and disposing of their own property by Representatives of their own choosing— if such is really the Case between Great Britain and her Colonies, then the connection between them ought to cease.

The Stamp Act Congress

So deep and widespread was the anger over the Stamp Act that the colonials organized the Stamp Act Congress to deal with the situation. Consisting of delegates from nine colonies, the Congress met in New York City from October 7–25 to work out a plan of action. They drew up a declaration of fourteen points that denounced the Stamp Act and declared that Americans were entitled "to the same inherent rights and liberties as the natural-born citizens of Great Britain and therefore could not be taxed without their consent."

The Sons of Liberty

A group of patriots who wanted more action than sending off petitions and hoping for good results joined together to form the Sons of Liberty. Theirs was a protest organization that cut across class lines, its members consisting of aristocrats, merchants, professionals, shopkeepers, craftsmen, and workers. The largest groups were made up of craftsmen and workers and the movement was called the "leather aprons" because this was their regular work garb.

The society got its name from Isaac Barre, an Englishman who had fought alongside Americans during the French and Indian Wars. During the debate on the Stamp Act in Parliament he argued against it and hailed the colonials as "Sons of Liberty." There were other members of Parliament who spoke out against the act.

The Sons of Liberty led the anti-Stamp Act movement in all the colonies and from the outset took the boldest action in defying it. At their first meeting they declared their rights and liberties, and while they also declared their firm adherence to the English constitution, they held themselves ready to defy the Stamp Act. They pledged to "go to the last extremity and venture life and fortunes to prevent the Stamp Act from ever taking place in the city and province," and then they warned people against selling or buying the stamps.

They promised to help any who broke this law:

> Resolved: that the persons who carry on business as formerly on *unstamped* paper shall be protected to the utmost power of this society.

They put up posters on walls, on trees, on fences, with this warning:

> The first man that either distributes or makes use of Stampt Paper, let him take care of his house, person and effects.
>
> *Vox Populi*

They got the unemployed to fill the streets to protest, and these were joined by sailors, artisans, and of course, the boys of the city added their shrill voices to the clamor. These demonstrations were a daily occurrence, with speeches on street corners, in taverns, on Bowling Green. The Sons of Liberty set up a liberty pole on the Fields, almost on the doorstep of the soldiers' barracks.

On October 28 the leading merchants signed an agreement to buy no more goods from England until the Stamp Act was repealed and to carry on business without using the stamps.

Citizens filled the streets of New York to protest the Stamp Act

The Sons of Liberty carried on correspondence with Sons in other colonies and saw to it that the "Stop buying British" campaign was carried out. The women played an important role during this time. They pledged not to purchase British goods and to buy clothing made in America from cloth made in America.

The *New York Gazette* printed in the largest type it owned "It is better to wear a homespun coat than to lose our liberty!"

The next English ship that anchored in the harbor had a cargo of salt, coal, and beer. The Sons went into action and back went the ship, its cargo unloaded.

When the first shipment of stamps arrived the Sons led a demonstration to the dock and threatened to seize and burn it. The soldiers had a rough time getting the stamps to safekeeping in Fort George.

On November 1, the day on which the Stamp Act became effective, the city went into mourning. Buildings were draped in black, shutters were drawn in houses and shops, flags were lowered to half mast, and muffled church bells tolled. Papers printed a skull in the place where the stamp should have been. The crowds poured into the streets shouting defiance. Speakers everywhere protested the "death of American liberties."

As night came the darkness failed to dampen spirits; torches and lanterns flared as the people gathered at the Fields to march to the fort where the stamps were. And as they marched they sang:

British soldiers had some difficulty getting the despised stamps to safekeeping in Fort George

With the beasts of the woods, we will ramble for food,
And lodge in wild deserts and caves.
And live poor as Job on the skirts of the globe,
Before we'll submit to be slaves, brave boys,
Before we'll submit to be slaves . . .

Several of the marchers had made an effigy of acting governor Cadwallader Colden. When they reached the fort, they set fire to the effigy. Word came that Colden was not at the fort so they seized his coach and burned it. They wrecked the home of the commander of the fort because he had boasted he would force the stamps down their throats with a sword. They stoned British troops.

New York was on the verge of rebellion. Cooler heads prevailed on the marchers to go home, but they vowed not to buy stamps, or allow others to do so.

The petitions sent by the Stamp Act Congress and other colonial groups were duly recorded in Parliament and then ignored. But they could not ignore the protests from their own merchants who were losing vast sums because of the American boycott. The Stamp Act had boomeranged on the British. This forced Parliament to repeal it.

New Yorkers celebrated when the news reached them. The Sons of Liberty paraded in triumph. Cannon was fired, church bells rang out the good news, and religious services of thanksgiving were held. Bonfires were made of the stamps, and so grateful were the members of the New York Assembly that they voted money for two statues—one of William Pitt who had worked for repeal and one of King George III.

In this struggle for their rights New Yorkers learned a lesson that was to serve them well in the troubled years ahead—that unity was strength and the boycott a weapon in their hands.

*When the Stamp Act
was repealed, bonfires were
made of the stamps in New York*

The Prendergast Rebellion

At this time the tenant farmers in upper New York were in a rebellious mood, too. They were in rebellion not against the Crown, but against their own landlords and their oppressive semifeudal system. They wanted the greater security of tenure (long or lifetime leases) and lower rents.

Some of the aristocrats who rented farms to them had great economic and political power that included manorial privileges such as the right to hold their own courts and punish tenants whom they thought guilty of wrongdoing.

Tenant farmers paid rent with a part of their harvest, their poultry, or sometimes cash, and a day or more service on their landlord's estate with a team of horses or oxen. When conditions were bad, as after a very poor harvest, a few tenants rebelled and did not allow the rent collector on their farms. The landlord then ordered the sheriff and soldiers either to force payment, arrest, or evict the farmers.

These farmers felt cheated; the landlords had gotten their vast lands as outright gifts or by bribing a governor with small sums of money. These lands would still be virgin forest had not the farmers turned them into food-producing acres. They knew that farmers in the other colonies owned the land they tilled and this was a sore point with them, for they had invested years of hard labor on the farm and did not even have the security of a long lease. Tenant uprisings broke out now and then and sometimes the neighboring farmers from Connecticut and Massachusetts came to their support.

In the 1760's the struggles broke out in Philipse Highland Patent, an estate of some two hundred thousand acres in Dutchess County. At that time the Wappinger Indians, led by their chief, Daniel Nimham, claimed ownership of nearly all the Philipse land on the basis that their title to

it had not yet ended. Some tenant farmers saw their opportunity to escape their semifeudal conditions and bought
titles from the Indians or accepted long leases from them.

The Stockbridge Indians began to make similar claims to
lands held by the Livingstons and the van Rensselaers, who
had about 750,000 acres on both sides of the Hudson River
near Albany. These claims were brought into court, which
was controlled by the great landowners and their friends.
The Indians lost.

The year 1766 had been a particularly bad year for the
farmers; a freezing winter and drought in the summer had
ruined their crops. If they gave the landlords the portion of
crops due them they would not have enough to feed their
families or enough seed for planting. One tenant complained to the other and Westchester and Dutchess counties
seethed with discontent.

When Philipse began to evict the tenants, one of them,
William Prendergast, who some years earlier had come from
Ireland, decided to take matters in hand. He went from
farmer to farmer and urged them to join him in a protest
to the governor. He organized over one thousand farmers
and they set out one morning in November on a march for
their rights and to improve their conditions of life.

But the landlords and merchants sent a swift horseman
to warn the governor. The farmers progressed slowly because they paused in the march to call out others to join
them.

As more tenants left their farms to join Prendergast, they
were seized and locked up in the Poughkeepsie jail. When
word of this reached Prendergast, he turned his men back.
They stormed the jail and freed the farmers.

This was rebellion against authority and the governor
acted quickly. He sent General Thomas Gage with three
hundred soldiers to disperse the tenants and to arrest Prendergast. He was placed on trial for high treason. His wife,

Mehitabel, who had supported him in all his efforts to organize the tenant farmers, sat beside him in court.

Prendergast was found guilty, sentenced to be executed in a gruesome way, and then hanged. His wife, although a Quaker, had developed some of the fighting qualities of her Irish-born husband. Immediately the verdict was announced, she leaped on her horse and galloped the eighty miles to New York City.

Arriving at the governor's house she insisted on seeing the governor himself. She pleaded her husband's case so convincingly that he ordered a delay in the execution and allowed her to send off an appeal to the king for a pardon.

Mehitabel rode back and arrived to find a crowd of farmers who had gathered at the jail to free their leader. She told them her news, and while they had doubts about a royal pardon, they obeyed her plea to return to their homes.

For William Prendergast the story ended happily—the king granted him a full pardon. But the rebellion did not improve conditions for the tenant farmers. Some of them left to settle in New Jersey where farms could be had for a small payment and without obligations to feudal landlords.

Others left to settle in the New Hampshire Grants where they later found themselves involved in the New York border troubles with these same landlords and with Ethan Allen and his Green Mountain Boys.

Chapter 8:

More Taxes and More Trouble

The resistance movement that had united the colonies had given the colonials a feeling that they were a power to be reckoned with. No longer would they submit meekly to laws that were unjust and limited them in their economic development.

Having appeased the colonials by repealing the Stamp Act, the British once again failed to read correctly the minds of "these raw backwoodsmen not unlike savages." In 1767 Parliament passed the Townshend Laws, which levied taxes on tea, glass, paper, lead, and paints. It also decreed that part of the revenue from this tax would pay the salaries of the governors and their officials.

The Colonial Assemblies objected to this; they had been paying these salaries directly. If the British government took over this function the colonists would have very little control over the actions of the governors.

The New York Assembly refused to obey one of the earlier laws—the Quartering Act—in which they had to provide housing and provisions for the British troops as well as cooking utensils, fuel, rum, cider, or vinegar to ward off scurvy. Parliament threatened to suspend the New York Assembly. The Assembly declared that Parliament did not have the right to stop it and went on governing.

Parliament proved that it had the right to stop it and ordered the royal governor not to sign legislation passed by the Assembly. This meant that legislation could not be put into effect. And there were enough British soldiers on hand to prevent the colonials from carrying out any law passed by the Assembly but not signed by the governor.

The Assembly then agreed to provide what was needed, but only by a majority of one. They had a sort of revenge in the kind of barracks they ordered built—and this did not endear the Americans to the British soldiers.

What angered the colonials even more than all these new laws were the Writs of Assistance that permitted an official to enter a home without a search warrant only on the suspicion that a law was being broken.

The Sons of Liberty went into action again. They organized protest meetings. When ships carrying customs officials and soldiers arrived to enforce the new laws, they were met by angry mobs.

Once again the boycott was put into use. On August 27, 1768, New York merchants and merchants of other colonies met and agreed not to purchase British goods after November 1 unless the taxes were repealed.

And, as before, the boycott boomeranged against the British. Their merchants convinced Parliament that they, and not the colonials, were the real losers. In April 1770 the Townshend Acts were repealed; only the tax on tea remained to prove to the colonies that Parliament was still in control.

In New York City the relations between the Sons of Liberty and the soldiers, which had been bad during the Stamp Act, now grew worse. There had been minor clashes between them. The officers were rowdy and insulting when drunk. One night they slashed some city lanterns with their swords; another time they attacked the night watch as well as a few colonials. A crowd gathered and it looked as if a riot would break out. General Gage was hurriedly sent for. It was the third time within a month that he was called on to curb his men.

The Sons had put up three liberty poles on the Fields and the soldiers had cut each one down. Now the fourth one was set in place and its base made secure with iron bands. On it was a sign reading: "George III, Pitt and Liberty." Patriots gathered around it to pledge themselves to freedom.

On the night of January 17, 1770, the soldiers managed to chop the pole down and left the pieces at the door of Montagne Tavern, a favorite meeting place for the Sons.

This was a challenge that could not be overlooked. The next afternoon the Sons attacked some soldiers on what is now John Street, which was then known as Golden Hill because it was a hilly field of golden wheat. Other soldiers rushed to the rescue of their comrades. The Sons had hard fists but the soldiers had swords. Several colonials were wounded and one died. This, New Yorkers claimed, was the first real bloodshed of the Revolution.

The statue of King George that the Assembly had ordered after the repeal of the Stamp Act arrived in August. Despite the resentment against the soldiers and the British, a group of colonial officials, clergy, and leading citizens attended the ceremonies that were held inside the fort.

When the procession of notables left the fort, the crowd outside fell in line behind them and marched across to Bowling Green where, on an imposing pedestal the gilded statue of the king, dressed as a Roman emperor, sat astride

The Sons of Liberty clashed violently with British soldiers over the destruction of the liberty pole

a horse. Here the New Yorkers honored the king in flattering speeches. (Only a few years later some of these New Yorkers were to pull down the same statue and melt it into bullets to be aimed at the same king's soldiers.)

The following two years were fairly quiet with only occasional clashes between the soldiers and the Sons of Liberty. Many New Yorkers thought that the Sons ought to disband now that the British had yielded to their demands.

But Parliament failed to learn through the experience of trial and error. The next blunder brought England and the American colonies still closer to war.

The Tea Party that Sparked a Revolution

In 1773 the British East India Company was given the monopoly of the tea trade and began to export tea to the colonies at a tax of three pence per pound. This was lower than the previous tax, making English tea less costly than the Dutch tea that some of the colonials smuggled. It should have pleased the colonials; instead, they roared out a loud, angry protest and formed committees to oppose the tax. This led to the events that caused the Revolution.

The trouble started when the East India Company began selling tea only through its own agents. This monopoly on tea threatened American tea merchants with ruin. The Sons of Liberty in all the colonies passed out leaflets stating that Americans "were determined not to be enslaved by any power on earth" and warned merchants not to store India tea in their warehouses.

Merchants in other trades became alarmed; if the tea trade was taken over entirely by the British, what other trade would be taken over next? Many merchants were ruined. Workers lost their jobs; the tea monopoly had reached down to the ordinary man and he had another gripe against the British.

The Sons of Liberty called for a boycott of any merchant who took tea from the East India Company. As before, its leaders were John Lamb, Isaac Sears, John Scott Morin, and the fiery-tongued Alexander MacDougal (who a few years later was to command one of the American regiments that seized Quebec). They had watchers at the harbor who sent out word when a British ship was seen approaching. It was boarded, and when the captain assured them that he had no tea aboard, they allowed the cargo to be unloaded.

Throughout the colonies the good dames stopped buying tea. It became the measure of one's patriotism not to serve it. They substituted sassafras or sage or the Dutch tea that was smuggled in.

On December 17, 1773, a ship carrying tea arrived in Boston harbor. Merchants, workers, and farmers disguised as Indians boarded the ship and dumped about $90,000 worth of tea into the waters. Paul Revere made the first of his famous rides that day; he brought news of the Tea Party to New York.

The Sons of Liberty could do no less than their Massachusetts compatriots; they boarded the first ship that reached New York waters, found that it had a cargo of tea and forced it to leave without unloading. The second ship, the *London,* arrived on April 22, 1774. The captain said he had no tea aboard. Skeptical, the Sons set to work and found eighteen chests of tea and then they had a tea party of their own. Into the waters went the tea and the captain narrowly escaped a dunking for his lie.

In Boston the governor, furious over the tea party, ordered more soldiers into the city. He demanded payment for the tea. The people refused to pay it.

The British government decided to prove that she still had the power to crush rebellion and that year—1774—

New Yorkers held public meetings denouncing the closing of Boston harbor

passed the Intolerable Acts. She would starve the people of Boston into obedience; one of these acts closed Boston harbor until all the dumped tea was paid for. Another act took away the power of the people to control their public affairs. Town meetings were banned and men accused of murder were ordered sent to England for trial. British soldiers were quartered in Massachusetts homes. The governor was removed for not being forceful enough and was replaced by General Gage.

New Yorkers held meetings to denounce these Acts. Money was raised for the people of Boston. Supplies of food were collected and sent to them and a flock of about 125 sheep were herded off to Boston.

Closing Boston harbor was a warning that the Sons of Liberty could not ignore and they kept the people roused against the British. New York merchants worried that what was happening in Boston could happen to them. Only a few years ago they had frowned on the activities of the Sons and wanted them to disband. Now they actively supported them.

The First Continental Congress

In January 1774, the New York Assembly kept the Committee of Correspondence busily in touch with other such colonial committees that, in turn, kept each other informed on the acts of the British in their area. And on May 15, the New York Committee proposed that all Colonial Committees of Correspondence meet in New York to work out a plan of action. At this time all the colonies except Georgia passed resolutions on the "Declaration of Rights" and arranged to send delegates to a meeting to be held in Philadelphia, which was more central than New York. This took place in September through October and was called the First Continental Congress. The first item discussed was cooperation and help for the people of Massachusetts. They sent off petitions to the British government to repeal the unjust laws, and as before, they knew that a boycott would be more effective than an appeal.

They formed the "Continental Association," which agreed not to import from nor export to Britain until American rights were restored. The delegates from New York voted against this nonimportation agreement because a large section of their colony was too loyal to England to join a boycott.

Loyalists, or Tories, as they were popularly called, were a strong faction in the New York Assembly. Some of them felt themselves more British than American. While other Tories had, in the beginning, approved the ideas of the

Sons of Liberty, they did not like the rowdy actions used to carry out these ideas. As the gap with the mother country widened, the Tories thought that Americans were recklessly steering the country toward independence. They wanted more freedom for the colonies and the Intolerable Acts repealed, but not at the expense of a revolution!

The First Continental Congress called on all the colonies to elect committees to carry out the work of the Continental Association. Only those who were strongly against the British agreed to work on these committees. It was evident to the Sons of Liberty that an increasing number of New Yorkers were moving closer to the Tory position. A Committee of Fifty-One was then organized to carry out the work of the Association. It was composed of patriots who differed in their political beliefs but were united against a common danger.

When the Continental Congress ended its sessions for 1774, all the delegates agreed to meet the next year—should conditions make it necessary. Nothing had been said about breaking ties with the mother country; it was, as yet, too drastic a step to consider.

The New York Assembly, which now was controlled by Tories, refused to send delegates to the Second Continental Congress. The Sons of Liberty then formed the Provincial Congress that was attended by delegates from the entire colony. It was to be a sort of "watch-dog" congress of the people. This congress elected delegates to the Second Continental Congress that was to meet in 1775.

Although the majority of New Yorkers were in a rebellious mood, there was still no popular demand for independence. The final step frightened many people; they had friends among British officials; soldiers were good for business; upstate farmers feared Indian attacks should the soldiers leave; New York merchants owned ships that plied the high seas, which the Royal Navy protected; and so on.

Then, too, wealthy merchants and landowners feared the democratic ideas of the Sons more than they hated British injustice. Their Tory activities did not go unnoticed by the Sons.

The patriots kept check on merchants who refused to carry out the boycott. The boys stoned their stores and had a good time doing what under normal conditions they would have been publicly whipped for.

More and more courts were opened to try people accused of breaking the Intolerable Acts, thus widening still more the split with the mother country.

The militia in every colony increased its numbers. Farmers and workers and even merchants began to train. They were dressed in homespun, for there was no money for uniforms, and many were without muskets. They drilled for a few weeks and then went back to their jobs, their shops, or their farms. A planter, George Washington, who had fought in the French and Indian Wars, would be put in charge of the combined militias when next the Continental Congress met.

In Massachusetts the "Minutemen" held themselves ready for any emergency. In Lexington, on April 19, 1775, a company of these men stood lined up outside the meeting-house ready to drill. With little cause or reason the British troops opened fire.

Paul Revere brought news of it and New Yorkers prepared to fight. Led by the Sons, the citizens took over City Hall and the Customs House. They seized the warehouses where British supplies were kept and took rifles and ammunition. Blacksmiths worked around the clock making rifles, workers began to train in the Fields.

The Sons had acted so quickly and forcefully because they knew that they faced a strong Tory party who would try to take over the city. (There were more Tories in New

The Sons of Liberty seized British military supplies

York than in any other colony, as was later revealed.) The Sons and their sympathizers declared that the Provincial Congress, and not the Assembly, was now the real government.

And then something happened on the New Hampshire Grants that bordered New York that gave the country the final nudge toward independence.

*Ethan Allen and the Green Mountain Boys
Go into Action*

Three weeks after Lexington, a group of frontiersmen on the New Hampshire Grants who were known as the Green Mountain Boys were called together by their leader, Ethan Allen, to discuss the common peril. They sat listening as he spoke of the strategic importance of Fort Ticonderoga and Crown Point.

Ethan Allen was a man of great daring and possessed of a soaring imagination. He proposed nothing less than that they seize these two forts for the American cause! The Boys were stunned; attack with rifles when the British had cannon! But Ethan was known to have done the impossible—they had done it with him, so they listened to his plan.

Ethan Allen had organized the Green Mountain Boys to protect the pioneers from eviction by the New York landlords who claimed title to the lands of these pioneers who earlier had bought them from the governor of the New Hampshire Grants. So effective were Allen and his Boys in punishing New York sheriffs and their deputies who tried to carry out the evictions that a large reward was offered for his capture, dead or alive.

At the same time that they were planning to attack, a New Haven merchant, Benedict Arnold, was also discussing the capture of these two forts with other colonials. They, too, saw the great importance of capturing them for the colonial cause. Benedict Arnold was commissioned to lead a party north to do this.

Benedict Arnold joined Ethan Allen and his eighty-three Green Mountain Boys. The frontiersmen in worn home-spun snickered at this "peacock" who was dressed in a handsome uniform with a shiny sword at his side and golden epaulettes at the shoulders, and topped off with a high, plumed hat. But they admired the military knowledge of this man who was later to betray his country.

The Second Continental Congress was then meeting in Philadelphia. Among the delegates were Samuel and John Adams, Benjamin Franklin, Thomas Jefferson, and George Washington. The seriousness of the situation called for the creation of a national army, and they appointed George Washington its commander-in-chief.

On May 10, at daybreak, the small force of the Green Mountain Boys surprised the British garrison at Fort Ticonderoga. When the British officer demanded to know on whose authority he was asked to surrender, Ethan Allen drew himself up to his full gigantic height and boomed out: "By the authority of Jehovah and the Continental Congress!"

Later, he sent a considerable portion of the captured army supplies to General Washington, who used it to force the British out of Boston.

Two days after this victory Seth Warner, another leader of the Green Mountain Boys, took Crown Point with all its supplies.

Benedict Arnold built a few ships and sailed down Lake Champlain and captured St. Johns, a strongly fortified British garrison.

These victories, Ethan Allen thought, would be of little consequence unless they carried the action into Canada. The bulk of the British Army was stationed there and was ready to invade the colonies to subdue the Americans. He

Ethan Allen surprised the British commander at Fort Ticonderoga

moved on into Canada and paused at a prearranged village to await the arrival of men and supplies. Either he was betrayed or his plans miscarried; he was captured by the British and sent off to England in chains.

In New York it was learned that the governor of Canada, Sir Guy Carleton, planned to retake Crown Point and Ticonderoga, and then move on to seize the colony's main city. To prevent this, New York troops, led by Colonel Alexander MacDougal, one of the leaders of the Sons of Liberty, moved north to fight. Under the command of General Richard Montgomery, they took Montreal in November. MacDougal had only about five hundred men when he went down the St. Lawrence River with Quebec as his objective. He was joined by Benedict Arnold who had about seven hundred men.

On December 31 they took Quebec.

In this battle General Montgomery was killed and Arnold wounded. It was a bitterly cold, windy day and a blinding snowstorm set in. The men, ragged with fighting their way through the rugged Maine wilderness, lacked supplies and food. An epidemic of smallpox broke out, and many died. The soldiers remained in Quebec all through the winter and then retreated to Crown Point. They had had no replacements for the dead and the sick, their supplies were exhausted, and they were in no condition to meet the fresh, well-equipped British soldiers who were now on their way to fight them in Quebec.

That year of 1775 the most pressing problem before the Provincial Congress in New York was weapons. Local committees collected arms and organized and drilled militia companies, and while all this activity seemed reassuring, the leaders knew that it was not enough to stand off an attack.

On June 27, people turned out in great numbers to greet General Washington who was on his way to take command of the Continental Army outside Boston. Later that same day the Tories turned out to greet Governor William Tryon, who was returning from a visit to England.

In August, when the New York troops began to remove the cannon from Fort George, the royal warship *Asia* opened fire. The troops returned the fire, killing one British soldier and wounding more.

The mood became so anti-British that on October 19 the acting governor, Tryon, fled to a British warship in the harbor.

Now the burning topic everywhere was independence. It divided families and friends. Among those who spoke out strongly in favor of it in New York were George Clinton, who became the first American governor of New York, John Jay, a later governor and the first Chief Justice of the United States, and Alexander Hamilton.

Although all the members of New York's Provincial

Congress were patriots, not al of them favored independence. On December 14, 1775, this Congress passed a resolution stating that resistance was the result of oppression by Parliament and that independence was not their goal.

New York, which then had a population of nearly twenty-two thousand, seemed to be splitting down the middle. A few aristocrats and wealthy merchants were for independence, as was the bulk of the workers, while a larger section of the aristocrats, merchants, and middle class was known to be Tories.

All New Yorkers faced the year 1776 with grim expectations; they knew that it would be the year of decision for all.

Chapter 9:

July 4, 1776!

While the news of Washington's gains on the Boston front was encouraging to the patriots, New Yorkers in general were worried by the victory. The general had succeeded in blockading General William Howe and his army inside that city, but they were being evacuated on British ships. Would they sail to New York and capture it?

News came that the Tories, led by the son of Sir William Johnson and joined by Indians, had attacked northern and western New York frontier settlements.

Encouraged by this, and the prospect of the arrival of the British Army, the Tories grew bolder and tried to influence people against independence. Their voice in the Provincial Congress grew stronger.

In Philadelphia the debates were still going on at the Second Continental Congress as to what course of action to take. At this time a pamphlet entitled *Common Sense* was written by Thomas Paine, a British subject who, believing in the American cause, had come here to speak out for it. He made a powerful argument for independence. Benjamin Franklin found this pamphlet so important that he kept his printing press busy making copies of it, and he helped to circulate them throughout the colonies.

Paine described the injustices that the colonials suffered and argued eloquently how to remove them. George Washington read the pamphlet and was strongly influenced by it as were many American leaders.

In New York the Sons of Liberty read the little pamphlet and passed it around. Now more and more of the prominent social families, some aristocrats among them, were coming over to the idea of independence. Groups in taverns discussed it, speakers on Bowling Green, on the Fields, and on street corners quoted at length from it, and the crowds roared their approval; they were through with petitions, with boycotts. Nothing less than independence would now satisfy them. *Common Sense* was creating a national spirit and a sense of national purpose.

As the British evacuated Boston and cut out to sea, General Washington, seasoned by his experiences as a soldier with the British Army during the French and Indian Wars, observed (and correctly too, as later events proved) that they were probably heading for Halifax for supplies and reinforcements and that they would then head south to seize New York.

He believed that the city, situated strategically at the mouth of the Hudson River, would be the base of operations for the British Army and Navy. He knew, too, that if New York were taken it would separate the New England colonies from the southern colonies, divide America, and thus make it easier for the British to conquer the country. "If the British take the city, they would stop the intercourse between the northern and southern colonies upon which depends the safety of America," he said.

It therefore was of the utmost urgency to see to New York defenses and he sent troops under General Charles Lee to begin preparations there.

Arriving in New York, General Lee made a study of these defenses, and then set men to work building fortifications on the Manhattan shoreline and on Brooklyn Heights that stretched along the upper bay. Barricades of logs were erected that crisscrossed the lower part of Manhattan from the Battery to Fort George.

In March the British completed their evacuation of Boston and one month later General Washington set out for New York. He arrived on April 13 at the head of five regiments and was escorted by the Philadelphia Light Horse. The militias of the thirteen colonies followed. He was met by nine militia companies of New York as he approached the city, and was welcomed by members of the Provincial Congress.

The streets were lined with cheering crowds and bells rang out to greet him. The odd assortment of clothes of the American Army must have amused the Tories among them; there were the gaunt, rugged northern frontiersmen in their fringed deerskin jackets and coonskin hats, the Pennsylvania regiment in brightly colored jackets, the more soberly clad Connecticut troops in homespun, and the short red coats and striped trousers of the New Jersey riflemen.

General Washington made his headquarters in Greenwich Village in the Richmond Hill mansion of the British paymaster-general. He inspected the fortifications and barricades made of old, used logs and scraps from worn-out and abandoned wharves. These had holes that had been filled with broken glass, rocks, and all kinds of odds and ends. He realized how poorly prepared for defense the city was.

And worse. There was a shortage of everything; of hous-

New Yorkers lined the streets to cheer the arrival of General Washington

ing, of supplies, of military engineers as well as skilled workers. And a woeful shortage of trained, experienced officers.

Now men were set to work building a chain of fortifications at the northern part of the city where Fort Tryon Park is now situated. It ran across the width of the island from the Hudson to the Harlem River. The section was hilly and gun emplacements were erected on the highest hills.

The Plot To Kill General Washington

A good general has the power to bring forward the best fighting qualities in a soldier and to deepen the patriotism of the citizens. General Washington had this quality of leadership. A quiet, rather reserved man of few words, he was, nevertheless, admired by the people. His success in forcing the mighty British Army out of Boston with an odd assortment of farmers and workers, planters and professional men, made him the first national hero of the country and so, to the Tories, he was the symbol of rebellion. Therefore he must be destroyed.

They set in motion a conspiracy to have him murdered. The Tories hoped at one stroke also to kill General Israel Putnam and other leaders and to seize the city.

This conspiracy was directed by Governor Tryon from the ship the *Dutchess of Gordon* on which he had taken refuge, and it included British officials and Tories. They wanted to end the war quickly by either capturing or killing American leaders, by destroying the army supplies, and by creating confusion and dissatisfaction in the American Army, which would lead to mutiny. The plot was exposed when one of General Washington's bodyguards was urged by two other guards to join them in the conspiracy. He immediately brought news of it to his commanding officer. That week a gunsmith, Gilbert Forbes, was arrested, but he refused to talk. He was given three days to reconsider and would then be executed if he maintained his silence. This threat had the desired results; Forbes talked and about twenty Tories were arrested. Those arrested were interrogated by the Committee of Examination which consisted of three officials who were sworn to secrecy. News of the plot was not revealed to the public at that time lest it cause confusion, fear, and panic.

Several officers did record the matter in their diaries, and we find that General Samuel B. Webb, General Washington's aide-de-camp entered in his journal on June 21, 1776:

> . . . the General received information that a most horrid plot was on foot by the vile Tories of this place and the adjacent towns and villages. Having taken the necessary precautions at two oclock in the morning, a number of officers and guards went to different places and took up many of their principals; among whom were David Matthews, Esq. Mayor of the city and to our great astonishment we find five or more of the General's life guard to be accomplices in the wicked scheme, which was at a con-

certed time, to assassinate His Excellency and the other
general officers, blow up the magazine, spike the cannon,
etc. It was to be put in execution as soon as the enemies
fleet appeared, if no proper time offered before; but,
thank God, they are discovered and many of them in close
custody, where I hope, they will receive the punishment
due such infamous wretches.

That month the British fleet of 130 ships containing ten
thousand men was strung along the outer waters of New
York harbor. At the end of June, General Howe arrived
and landed his troops, which now included Hessians (Germans), on Staten Island. They were fully equipped and
seasoned in battle. The entire force now consisted of 31,000
men. Out in the harbor rode the ships of the British Royal
Navy commanded by Admiral Richard Howe. He was await-
ing orders to form a blockade around the island.

With spyglasses the American officers could see the
British drilling. They had bright new uniforms and each
one had a musket. The men of the Continental Army lacked
uniforms, lacked weapons and powder. The British Army
and particularly the Germans drilled with precision and
looked like toy mechanical soldiers. Experienced in fighting
Indians and in hunting, the Americans were not good at
drilling. Frontiersmen were very individualistic and independent and not used to having orders barked at them or
to marching in close, even lines. But they knew how to
run forward at the enemy, knew expertly how to use a rifle,
and most important of all, they knew for what they were
fighting.

The work of defense went on feverishly. More shore
batteries were set up on Governor's Island as well as along
the shores of Brooklyn and Queens. They blocked off the
Hudson to the British by sinking a few old and unusable
ships and these they had heavily weighted so that they

would maim the British ships and stop them. Gunfire would then blast away at them from the batteries at Fort Lee on the New Jersey side and from Fort Washington on the Manhattan side.

The patriots were very optimistic. The commander-in-chief did not allow himself to be pessimistic, although news had just been brought that Sir Guy Carleton was preparing an invasion of upstate New York and that General Howe would sail part of the army up the Hudson and the two forces would meet in Albany.

On June 7, at the Second Continental Congress, the matter of independence was being seriously discussed. Richard Henry Lee of Virginia offered a resolution that "These United Colonies are and of right ought to be free and independent states; that they are absolved from all allegiance to the British Crown; and that all political connection between them and the State of Great Britain is, and ought to be totally dissolved."

A committee headed by Thomas Jefferson was set up to consider this resolution and the Congress set up a committee of five to prepare a declaration.

When it was written and offered, the debates in Congress lasted for days, thus delaying the final vote, for every delegate knew that the price of independence was war; that it would turn the colonials from subjects of Great Britain to its enemies. It was the gravest decision in all their lives. Each signer of the Declaration of Independence knew that in signing he was also signing his own death warrant if the colonies lost the war.

The Declaration of Independence

On Thursday, July 4, 1776, the Declaration written by Thomas Jefferson was voted on and adopted by twelve of the thirteen colonies. The New York delegates had been instructed not to vote on it as a new provincial government was then being elected.

On July 9 the newly elected Provincial Congress met in the courthouse at White Plains and approved the Declaration.

On July 9, too, a horseman bearing a copy of the Declaration rode into New York and handed it to General Washington. He drew his soldiers up at the Fields and the document was read to the troops and the crowd that had assembled.

> . . . we hold these truths to be self-evident; that all men are created equal; that they are endowed by their Creator with certain unalienable rights; that among these are life, liberty and the pursuit of happiness. That, to secure these rights, governments are instituted among men, deriving their just powers from the consent of the governed . . .

Americans All

The soldiers made a square in the center of which, tall and imposing on his white horse, sat the commander-in-chief. Beyond, and all about, were the listening people.

Each officer who stood at attention knew that if the British won the war he would be captured and would suffer a traitor's fate—death by hanging.

It was an awesome and very solemn moment in all their lives.

One wonders what thoughts passed through the mind of their general as he listened to these stirring words. He was realist enough to know that the odds at that moment were in Britain's favor; that of the three million Americans in the land many were Tories; that England was the greatest power on earth; that she had the wealth, the resources, the trained officers; that the Royal Navy was master of the seas

In CONGRESS, July 4, 1776.

The unanimous Declaration of the thirteen united States of America.

The New York delegates, William Floyd, Philip Livingston, Francis Lewis, and Lewis Morris, added their signatures to the Declaration of Independence at the top of the fifth column and could prevent other nations from helping the colonies.

While a commander must be a realist he cannot allow himself to dwell only on the negative side, and so Washington must have thought of the advantages the Americans had; the long eastern seacoast dotted with villages and towns from whose midst had come volunteers to serve the cause of independence, and that these, together with the people living inland, were very patriotic. The British were strangers to this territory and would not obtain help of any kind from them.

Besides, ships from England made the three thousand-mile voyage to America in two months when there were no storms; the British would have a serious supply problem on their hands.

And, as was proven during the French and Indian Wars, British soldiers were not good at fighting in the dense woods while the Americans were familiar with and knew how to use the forests to their advantage. And most important, Americans had deep convictions about freedom and the will and the courage to fight to defend it.

The immigrants from Europe who had become frontiersmen there, who had hacked out farms, villages, and cities from these forests, had, in the doing, developed a sense of freedom, a sense that they counted for something as human beings. The Europeans who kept coming absorbed this new thought and atmosphere. It acted upon them so that in time a new breed was produced—the American. They followed Washington through the long and bitter struggle that ended in victory and independence.

Bibliography

BEARD, CHARLES A. and MARY R., *The Rise of American Civilization*. New York: Macmillan, 1942.

BECKER, CARL LOTUS, *Political Parties in the Province of New York, 1760–1776*. Madison: University Press of Wisconsin, 1960.

BLIVEN, JR., BRUCE, *Battle for Manhattan*. New York: Henry Holt, 1955.

BROWN, HENRY COLLINS, *Story of Old New York*. New York: E. P: Dutton & Co., Inc., 1934.

COTTON, JULIA M., *Annals of Old Manhattan*. New York: Brentano (in cooperation with The New-York Historical Society), 1901.

EARLE, ALICE MORSE, *Colonial Days of Old New York*. Port Washington, N.Y.: Ira J. Friedman, Inc., 1962.

ELDRIDGE, PAUL, *Crown of Empire*. New York: Thomas Yoseloff, Inc., 1957.

ELLIS, DAVID M., FROST, JAMES A., SYRETT, HORACE C., and CARMAN, HARRY J., *A History of New York*. Ithaca: Cornell University Press (in cooperation with The New-York Historical Society), 1957.

ELLIS, DAVID M., FROST, JAMES A., and FINK, WILLIAM R., *New York, The Empire State*. Englewood Cliffs, N.J.: Prentice Hall, 1961.

ELLIS, EDWARD ROBB, *The Epic of New York City*. New York: Coward-McCann, Inc., 1966.

EMERSON, CAROLINA D., *New York City Old and New*. New York: E. P. Dutton & Co., Inc., 1953.

LYMAN, SUSAN E., *Story of New York*. New York: Crown Publishers, 1964.

VAN LOON, HENDRIK, *Life and Times of Peter Stuyvesant*. New York: Henry Holt, 1928.

WHEELER, MARY A., *New York State Yesterday and Today*. New York: Charles Scribner's Sons, 1935.

I want to think Miss Nancy Hale, Librarian at The New-York Historical Society, for her help in putting records and source books at my disposal.

Important Dates

1526—Estavan Gomez reached the site of New York.

1609—Henry Hudson sailed into New York harbor.

1614—The Dutch built a trading post on Manhattan Island and another at Fort Orange (now Albany).

1626—Peter Minuit, the first governor of New Netherland, arrived in Manhattan.

1633—The first church was built in New Amsterdam.

1647—Peter Stuyvesant became governor of New Amsterdam.

1664—New Amsterdam was taken over by the English and was renamed New York.

1673—The first regular mail service between Boston and New York was started.

—New York was reclaimed by the Dutch and renamed New Orange.

1674—England and Holland signed a peace treaty, of which one of the provisions was the return of New Orange to British control. The colony was again renamed New York.

1683—The first General Assembly was held at Fort James.

1689—France declared war on England.

1690—French and Indian forces destroyed Schenectady by fire.

—The first Congress of American colonies met in New York to plan a common defense against the French.

1725—William Bradford began publishing the first newspaper in New York—a weekly called the *New York Gazette*.

1733—John Peter Zenger started publishing the *New York Weekly Journal*.

1754—King's College, now Columbia University, was founded.

—The final struggle began between France and England for control of American territory.

1763—The French and Indian Wars ended.

1764—Parliament passed the Sugar Act, taxing American colonies for all sugar imports.

1765—Parliament passed the Billeting or Quartering Act, making the colonies provide barracks, bedding, and fuel for English soldiers in America.

—Parliament passed the Stamp Act, requiring the colonies to purchase stamps for all newspapers, licenses, and various legal documents.

—The Stamp Act Congress met in New York to denounce the Stamp Act and to work out a plan of action to have it abolished.

1766—The Stamp Act was repealed.

1767—Parliament passed the Townshend Acts levying taxes on tea, glass, paper, lead, and paints.

1770—The Townshend Acts were repealed.

1774—The First Continental Congress was held in Philadelphia.

1775—The Second Continental Congress met in Philadelphia.

1776—The Declaration of Independence was voted on and adopted on July 4.

—The Declaration of Independence was signed on August 2.

Places To Visit

Visitors to New York may wish to visit some of these historical sites:

AMSTERDAM

OLD FORT JOHNSON. On this site stands the restored former home of Sir William Johnson, British Colonial Indian Commissioner. Built in 1749, it is now a museum of Indian and colonial artifacts. July-August, Tuesday-Saturday, 10 A.M.–5 P.M.; Sunday, Monday, from 1 P.M.; May-June, September-October, daily from 1 P.M.; closed November-April. Adults, 50¢; under 12, free with adult.

AUBURN

CAYUGA MUSEUM OF HISTORY AND ART. Indian, pioneer, early American and Civil War relics are on exhibit in an original 1791 log cabin. Art shows change regularly. Tuesday-Friday, 1–5 P.M.; Saturday, 9 A.M.–noon, 1–5 P.M.; Sunday, 2–5 P.M.; closed January 1, May 30, July 4, Thanksgiving, December 25. Free.

OWASCO STOCKADED INDIAN VILLAGE. Exhibits of Iroquoian art can be seen at the site of this original Indian settlement. Demonstrations are given of Indian activities from the tenth century. Mid-June–mid-October, daily, 10 A.M.–6 P.M.; closed rest of year. Adults, 50¢; children, 25¢.

BAY SHORE, LONG ISLAND

SAGTIKOS MANOR. On the night of April 21, 1790, George Washington lodged here. His bed, as well as the original kitchen, dining room, and parlor are on display. July-August, Tuesday and Thursday, 1–4 P.M.; May 15–June and September. By appointment. Closed rest of year. Adults, 50¢; children, 25¢.

CANAJOHARIE

FORT PLAIN RESTORATION AND MUSEUM. This important Revolutionary War post was built in 1776 and razed in 1786. On the grounds are a colonial and Indian Museum and a Mohawk Indian cemetery. Restoration of the fort and field restoration is planned. Field archaeology is in progress. May 30–Labor Day, daily, 10 A.M.– 5 P.M.; closed rest of year. Adults, 50¢; under 12, free.

CATSKILL

BRONCK HOUSE MUSEUM (1663). Built by Pieter Bronck, son of Jonas Bronck, whose 500-acre *bouwerie* became New York City's Bronx. A brick house dating from 1738 and a thirteen-sided barn adjoin other buildings. Indian artifacts, pottery and vehicles are on display. There is also a picnic grove. May 15–September, Tuesday-Saturday, 1 A.M.–5 P.M.; Sunday, 2–6 P.M.; closed rest of year. Adults, $1; 12–16, 25¢; under 12, free. The Pieter Bronck Trading Post deals in antiques, July-August, daily except Monday; May-June, September, weekends only; closed rest of year.

HAGUE

LAKE GEORGE BATTLEFIELD STATE PARK. Ruins of Fort George stand on the site of the Battle of Lake George (1755). Picnic tables, fireplaces, charcoal grills, and water are available for picnickers. May 30–second Sunday in September, daily, 9 A.M.–10 P.M. Standard fee.

HERKIMER

This fort, settled by Palatines, was raided by Indians during the French and Indian War. From here General Nicholas Herkimer marched to the bloody Revolutionary War Battle of Oriskany on August 4, 1777.

MANHATTAN

THE NEW-YORK HISTORICAL SOCIETY at 170 Central Park West houses a rich variety of exhibits on American history with emphasis on New York. Duncan Phyfe's tool chest, Washington's camp cot, Audubon watercolor drawings, volunteer fire department, various memorabilia, American folk art, glass. Research library open daily except Sunday, 10 A.M.–5 P.M.; holidays from 1 P.M.; August, open Monday-Friday only; adults only. Museum open Tuesday-Friday, Sunday 1–5 P.M.; Saturday from 10 A.M. Closed August. Building closed January 1, May 30, July 4, Labor Day, Thanksgiving, December 25. Free.

MUSEUM OF THE CITY OF NEW YORK, 1220 Fifth Avenue between East 103 and 104 Streets. An excellent museum on the history of New York City and its port, with dioramas, ship models, material on theatrical history, fire fighting, costumes and other phases of this city's life. Dutch Gallery. Adults, 25¢; children with adult, 10¢; acoustiguide tour, 50¢ extra. Covers life in the early Dutch settlement; reconstructed portion of Fort Amsterdam. Walking tours of the city from mid-April–mid-October. Fee. Request brochure for dates. Free Sunday concerts October-April; adults and older children. Tuesday-Saturday, 10 A.M.–5 P.M.; Sunday, holidays from 1 P.M.; closed December 25; closed. Monday except holidays, then closed Tuesday. Free.

DYCKMAN HOUSE AND MUSEUM (1783), Broadway and 204th Street. The only eighteeth-century farmhouse still on Manhattan Island. Built by William Dyckman, it has been refurnished with some original Dyckman pieces and others of the period; gives a good picture of daily living at that time. Daily except Monday, 11 A.M.–5 P.M. Free.

MONTICELLO

FORT DELAWARE. A replica of the 1754 stockade, cabins, blockhouses and other buildings house various exhibits. Life of early settlers is depicted by the costumed staff. 10 A.M.–6 P.M.: July-August, daily; May 30–June, September, weekends only; closed rest of year. Adults, $1.25; 8–16, 60¢; 7 years and under, free with parents.

OYSTER BAY, LONG ISLAND

RAYNHAM HALL, 20 West Main Street. Bought and enlarged by Samuel Towsend in 1738, this was the scene of intrigue among the Colonials before and during the Revolution; Victorian wing added in 1851. Authentically restored, furnished with eighteenth-century and Victorian pieces; eighteenth-century garden. Monday, Wednesday-Saturday, 10 A.M.–Noon, 1–5 P.M., Sunday from 1 P.M.; closed January 1, Thanksgiving, December 25. Adults, 50¢; under 12, free with adult. No spike heels.

RIVERHEAD, LONG ISLAND

SUFFOLK COUNTY HISTORICAL SOCIETY, West Main Street. Artifacts of early life in the county—country store, blacksmith shop, carriage room with old fire fighting apparatus; farm implements, Indian exhibits; Children's Corner with dolls and games. Monday-Saturday except holidays, 1–5 P.M. Free.

SHELTER ISLAND

Quakers persecuted by the Puritans in New England settled

Shelter Island, in Gardiners Bay just off the east end of Long Island. The island is reached by ferries from Greenport, on the north fork of Long Island, or from North Haven, on the south. There is a monument to the Quakers and a graveyard with seventeenth-century stones. The island has many summer homes; also swimming, fishing, boating and golfing.

STATEN ISLAND

RICHMONDTOWN. Restoration of more than thirty pre-Revolutionary sites is in progress. Several have been completed: Voorlezer's House (1695), Kings Road, oldest known elementary school building in the U.S. 25¢. Lake-Tysen House, Kings Road, 25¢. Stephens Store, Court Place and Center Street, 10¢. April-October, Saturday, Sunday, 2–5 P.M. Closed rest of year. Children free.

TARRYTOWN

PHILLIPSBURG MANOR, in North Tarrytown, west of US 9, two miles north of Dewey Thruway Exit 9. Seventeenth-century home of Frederick Philipse, merchant and landowner. Restored operating grist mill.

WHITEHALL

SKENESBOROUGH MUSEUM, Boulevard, US 4, NY 22, former Canal Terminal Building memorializes first ships built and used for defense of U.S. in 1775–1776. Models of first U.S. Navy Yard, canal, locks, USS *Saratoga;* Admiral P. Potter room with memorabilia; doll room; hulk of USS *Ticonderoga,* raised from lake in 1958; local history exhibits, War of 1812 and Revolutionary War artifacts. Last week in June–Labor Day, daily, 10 A.M.–5 P.M.; rest of year by appointment. Adults, 60¢; children, 25¢, free with adult.

WHITE PLAINS

WASHINGTON'S HEADQUARTERS (1680), Virginia Road in North White Plains. Restored; Revolutionary War relics; lectures. February 22–December 15, Tuesday-Saturday, 10 A.M.–4 P.M. Sunday from 1 P.M. Closed rest of year. Free.

MONUMENT, South Broadway and Mitchell Place. Here the Declaration of Independence was adopted July 4, 1776, and the state of New York formally organized.

Times and admission fees may change without notice.

Index

New York Colony, eductaion in, 69–71; immigration in, 65–67; mail delivery in, 74–75; social classes in, 67–69
New York Gazette, 59, 91, 94
New York Weekly Journal, 61
Nicholls, Richard, 36, 37, 39, 40
Nicholson, Francis, 44, 45, 46–47
Nimham, Daniel, 98

Oneida Indians, 82
Onodonga Indians, 4
Oxford, Earl of, 54

Paine, Thomas, 118
Philadelphia Light Horse, 120
Philipse, Frederick, 45, 48, 54, 98
Philipse Highland Patent, 98
Pig (ship), 9
Piracy, 52, 53–54, 56
Pitt, William, 85, 96, 103
Plymouth Colony, 12, 48
Portugal, 5, 6
Prendergast, Mehitabel, 100
Prendergast, William, 99–100
Prendergast Rebellion, 98–100
Prideaux, John, 87
Princeton University, 69
Protestants, 48
Provincial Congress, 109, 112, 115, 116, 117, 120, 124
Putnam, Israel, 85, 121

Quakers, 32, 68, 69

Raritan Indians, 21–22
Rattle Watch, 74
Restless (ship), 8
Revere, Paul, 105, 110
Rhode Island Colony, 48
Roelantsen, Adam, 13

Saint Nicholas Church, 19
Schaghen, Peter Jans, 15
Scots, 13
Sears, Isaac, 105
Second Continental Congress, 109, 113, 117, 123

Seneca Indians, 4
Sheep (ship), 9
Shirley, William, 82, 83
Sloughter, Henry, 48, 49, 50
Smith, William, 63
Smits, Claes, 22
Smuggling, 52–53
Sons of Liberty, 92, 93, 94, 95, 96, 102–06 *passim,* 108, 109, 110, 114, 118
Stadt Huys (City Hall), 29, 37
Stamp Act, 91, 92, 93, 95, 96, 101, 103
Stamp Act Congress, 92, 96
Stockbridge Indians, 99
Stuyvesant, 26–29, 30–32, 34–35, 36–38, 40
Stuyvesant, Balthazar, 37
Sugar Act, 88, 89, 91
Supreme Council, 26

Tiger (ship), 8
Tories, *see* Loyalists
Townshend Laws, 101
Trinity Church, 69
Tryon, William, 115, 121–22

Van Cortland, Stephen, 45, 48, 49
Van Dam, Rip, 59
Van Rensselaer, Kiliaen, 17, 99
Van Twiller, Wouter, 16–17
Vespucci, Amerigo, 80
Virginia Colony, 80
Virginia Provincial Militia, 82

Walloons, 9, 11
Wappinger, Indians, 98
Warner, Seth, 113
Warren, Peter, 78
Washington, George, 80, 110, 113, 115, 117, 118, 119, 120, 121, 122, 124, 126
Webb, Samuel B., 122
Weekquaesgeek Indians, 22
William III (of England), 44, 48, 54
Writs of Assistance, 102

Yale University, 69

Zenger, John Peter, 61–64